Daily Redemption

Daily Encouragement for Right Choices

JACK A. MADSON

WESTBOW
PRESS®
A DIVISION OF THOMAS NELSON
& ZONDERVAN

WestBow Press books may be ordered through booksellers or by contacting:

WestBow Press
A Division of Thomas Nelson & Zondervan
1663 Liberty Drive
Bloomington, IN 47403
www.westbowpress.com
844-714-3454

Scripture quotations taken from The Holy Bible, New International Version® NIV®
Copyright © 1973 1978 1984 2011 by Biblica, Inc. TM.
Used by permission. All rights reserved worldwide.

ISBN: 978-1-6642-0298-6 (sc)
ISBN: 978-1-6642-0297-9 (hc)
ISBN: 978-1-6642-0299-3 (e)

Library of Congress Control Number: 2020916042

Print information available on the last page.

WestBow Press rev. date: 09/23/2020

DEDICATION

I would like to dedicate this work to my six grandsons and their parents, who have done an outstanding job of raising their kids with life principles and Christian beliefs.

I can barely imagine the challenges parents face with their children entering into the secular world in this day and age.

I trust my grandsons will continue their walk of faith as they enter into the age of accountability. May this book be another tool to help guide and build their faith with these daily exercises. I list their first names here in the order of age; Taylor, Andrew, Preston, Caden, Will, and Sawyer.

Like any strength-building action, it requires repetition and perseverance.

"For this reason, make every effort to add to your faith goodness; and to goodness, knowledge; and to knowledge, self-control; and to self-control, perseverance; and to perseverance, godliness; and to godliness, brotherly love" (2 Peter 1:5-7).

"For if you possess these qualities in increasing measure, they will keep you from being ineffective and unproductive in your knowledge of our Lord Jesus Christ. But if anyone does not have them, he is near-sighted and blind and has forgotten that he has been cleansed from his past sins" (2 Peter 1:8-9).

Also, I want to dedicate this to my oldest son, Joshua, who is stricken with health challenges. He has battled this for many years, wondering "why is this happening to me"? He clings to his faith, and the Lord Jesus has protected him. He is in a better place now, in a living situation with medication. One day he will dance with the angels in heaven who looked over him. His face will radiate will gladness and joy, and we will all praise the Lord.

My wife has stood with me through the good, bad, and the ugly of life. We have fought hard for our marriage, now of over 50 years. Half the marriages don't make it, and devastation on our families is painful. We honor the Lord for how he preserved us through it all, and as we enter into our senior years. We hold on tight to the heritage of our faith and the deep roots of goodness and beauty we see in each other. This, along with the everlasting joy and peace of our families, we press on.

"Trust in the Lord with all your heart and lean not on your own understanding: In all your ways acknowledge him and he will make your paths straight. Do not be wise in your own eyes: fear the Lord and shun evil. This will bring health to your body and nourishment to your bones. Honor the Lord with your wealth, with the firstfruits of all your crops: then your barns will be filled to overflowing, and your vats will brim over with new wine."
(Proverbs 3:5-10)

CONTENTS

by Pastor Don Brekhus

It is a privilege and an honor for me to write a short introduction to the devotional written by Jack Madson. He and his family have been our friends and neighbors for three generations. Jack has written a powerful daily devotional that is both simple and profound. His insights are drawn from a lifetime of experiences. He, like Moses, David, and Paul, have been on the mountaintop as well as in the valley. These experiences are both humbling and life-changing moments where he experiences the grace of God.

Madson is a gifted word-smith, with short phrases and sentences in which he expresses deep spiritual truths. Jack is able to take a Bible verse and in a few words open it up so it becomes alive and active. Secondly, he expresses our helplessness and brokenness as sinful, desperate people, then presents the good news, that Jesus makes us whole and gives us peace.

It is my prayer that the Holy Spirit will bless all of us who read these devotionals, that these scriptures and insights will bring praise to God, strengthen the believers and expand His Kingdom in our midst.

I highly recommend this Daily Devotional to everyone, including skeptics, doubters, new Christians, as well as those who have journeyed in the faith.

Sincerely in Christ,
Pastor Don Brekhus

Being a Christian is not easy... but it's simple.

My journey is not unlike many, a battle of wills - mine and the Lord's. I see, and I long for this Lord, but then my inner self-calls for selfish needs - that at the seed are sinful and wrong. Surrender is all that He asks, obedience and longing for a loving relationship. I cry out, Lord helps me to not be a prisoner to myself.

My life had reached a crisis and the Lord said this is enough! Get right with me, your wife, your family, your friends, and stop living this life of lies and double standards. He put me on this project to create these "panels" about who I am when I'm one with Him and when I'm not. It's a process of daily redemption or becoming "redemptionated" and holy.

Battle Lines and Footholds.....

The enemy is relentless, patient, full of deception, and wanting nothing short of our deliverance to hell eternally. This "test" of life promises to be the most incredible investment in a time and place we will ever experience. The self-directed will is strong, desiring self-serving satisfaction immediately. The enemy knows our weaknesses and digs in, gaining a "foothold" and building strength. God is stronger and will come to our defense. As we draw near to God, He will draw near to us and give us strength! As we get to know the Lord, He will purify us and remove the "footholds" of sin. Our lives will become free from the bondage and guilt of sin. These 365 days of devotion are about a God who loves each one of us so much and wants to give us this freedom and love - Praise God!

God Is

Without God I am

With God I am

February 3 – God is Disciplined

February 4 – God is Worthy

February 5 – God is Forever

February 6 – God is Living

February 7 – God is Teacher

February 8 – God is Righteous

February 9 – God is Judge

February 10 – God is Divine

February 11 – God is Authority

February 12 – God is Redeemer

February 13 – God is Faithful

February 14 – God is Holy

February 15 – God is Presence

February 16 – God is Free

February 17 – God is Peace

February 18 – God is Righteous

February 19 – God is Alpha & Omega

February 20 – God is Almighty

February 21 – God is Lord

February 22 – God is Rejoicing

February 23 – God is Protection

February 24 – God is Justice

February 25 – God is Salvation

February 26 – God is Comforter

February 27 – God is Life

February 28 – God is Protector

February 29 – God is Love

March 1– God is Adequacy

March 2 – God is Determined

March 3 – God is Awesome

March 4 – God is Pure

March 5 – God is Goodness

March 6 – God is Compassionate

March 7 – God is Gracious

April 11 – God is Cleansing
April 12 – God is Eternal
April 13 – God is Savior
April 14 – God is Affirmation
April 15 – God is Coming
April 16 – God is Exalted
April 17 – God is Spirit
April 18 – God is Fair Minded
April 19 – God is Giving
April 20 – God is Deserving
April 21 – God is Reason
April 22 – God is Reigning
April 23 – God is Accomplished
April 24 – God is Caring
April 25 – God is a Companion
April 26 – God is a King
April 27 – God is A Rock
April 28 – God is Glory
April 29 – God is The Way
April 30 – God is Present
May 1 – God is Timeless
May 2 – God is Wise
May 3 – God is Dependable
May 4 – God is Perfect
May 5 – God is Appointing
May 6 – God is Rescuer
May 7 – God is Defender
May 8 – God is Omnipresent
May 9 – God is Caring
May 10 – God is Independent
May 11 – God is Obedient
May 12 – God is a Servant
May 13 – God is Holy Spirit
May 14 – God is Jesus Christ

May 15 – God is Regimented
May 16 – God is Unity
May 17 – God is Whole
May 18 – God is Omnipotent
May 19 – God is Courage
May 20 – God is Triumphant
May 21 – God is Complete
May 21 – God is Complete
May 22 – God is Great
May 23 – God is Leading
May 24 – God is Granting
May 25 – God is Valuable
May 26 – God is with Me
May 27 – God is a Messenger
May 28 – God is Calling
May 29 – God is Changing Us
May 30 – God is Saving Us
May 31 – God is Tending To Us
June 1 – God is Ministering to Us
June 2 – God is Reconciling Us
June 3 – God is Listening
June 4 – God is Watching
June 5 – God is Fullness
June 6 – God is Pardoning Us
June 7 – God is a Pit Stop
June 8 – God is Amazing
June 9 – God is Here
June 10 – God is Ambitious
June 11 – God is Changing Our Desires
June 12 – God is Grieved
June 13 – God is Touching Our Lives
June 14 – God is Amending
June 15 – God is a Shelter
June 16 – God is a Calming Us

June 17 – God is a Teaching Us
June 18 – God is Cleansing Us
June 19 – God is Keeping Me from Myself
June 20 – God is Restoring Us
June 21 – God is Helping Us
June 22 – God is Pruning Us
June 23 – God is Bread
June 24 – God is Quieting Us
June 25 – God is Instructing Us
June 26 – God is Purifying Us
June 27 – God is Immortal Hope
June 28 – God is With Us
June 29 – God is Reconciling Us
June 30 – God is Giving Our Lives Meaning
July 1– God is Pardoning Us
July 2 – God is Relieving Us
July 3 – God is Life to the Mind - Renewal
July 4 – God is Health for the Body
July 5 – God is Mine
July 6 – God is Sufficient
July 7 – God is Angry
July 8 – God is Happy
July 9 – God is Listening
July 10 – God is Refreshing Us
July 11– God is Easy
July 12– God is Inspiring Us
July 13 – God is Walking With Us
July 14 – God is Purging Us
July 15 – God is Offering Us
July 16 – God is Filling Us
July 17 – God is Lightening Us
July 18 – God is Affirming Our Purpose
July 19 – God is Hearkening Us
July 20 – God is Our Advocate

July 21 – God is Immanent

July 22 – God is Everywhere

July 23 – God is Setting Us Free

July 24 – God is Growing Us Slowly

July 25 – God is Helping Us

July 26 – God is Cleaning Up Our Mess

July 27 – God is In Control

July 28 – God is Giving Me Sight

July 29 – God is An Anchor

July 30 – God is To Be Feared

July 31 – God is Cherishing Us

August 1 – God is With Me

August 2 – God is Unseen

August 3 – God is Fulfilling Us

August 4 – God is Concerned

August 5 – God is Breaking The Chains

August 6 – God is The Answer

August 7 – God is Reviving

August 8 – God is Enabling Us

August 9 – God is No Insurance Policy

August 10 – God is Hurt

August 11 – God is Wanting Us to Commit

August 12 – God is Not Cheap

August 13 – God is Big

August 14 – God is Getting Our Attention

August 15 – God is Bringing Us Back

August 16 – God is Overhauling Us

August 17 – God is Serious

August 18 – God is Our Treasure

August 19 – God is Wanting Fruit

August 20 – God is Measuring Our Pain

August 21 – God is a Flavorful Taste

August 22 – God is Holding Us

August 23 – God is Keeping Us

God Is....

The Bible speaks of this amazing Being, who He is, how He thinks about His children, what He has done, and how he wants us to live - now and forever.

Without God I am....

Given to myself, I serve my endless needs, my nature puts me on the throne, my desires have no limits, but in the end, my life is meaningless - yet accomplished. My complacent ignorance of God is my capstone.

With God I am.....

Now I have experienced His might, healing touch, and His transforming power is making sense the true meaning of why He created me. I'm at peace with myself, my God, and my world, but purposeful and driven to be all He planned for me to be and do.

Daily Redemption – "redemptionate"

To coin a new word – "redemptionate", meaning to restore a relationship with my creator and redeemer. Jesus Christ died once for all, and is calling each to a new and better connection, daily. We learn to love the giver, not the gifts.

1. Godly Attribute: Contemplate the verse and supportive scripture around the characteristic of God. Conduct your own searches to find other supportive verses.
2. Internalize the verse, what is it saying to you? Write down your thoughts.
3. When you look at this attribute and place it on yourself, how do you strive to embrace it selfishly without God?
4. When you look at this attribute and place it on yourself, how do you strive to embrace it when you partner with God, the Lord Jesus Christ?
5. Internalizing all this, what action steps will you take today to embrace this attribute? Think about this attribute throughout the day, and jot down notes to yourself as to how the Lord helped you. Where did he show up?
6. Make sure to thank him when you turn the lights out at the end of the day! You will be blessed!!!

"Set your minds on things above, not on earthly things" (Colossians 3:2).

JANUARY 1 – GOD IS POWERFUL

The Bible says, "The LORD is slow to anger and great in power; the LORD will not leave the guilty unpunished. His way is in the whirlwind and the storm, and clouds are the dust of his feet" (Nahum 1:3).

Powerful – All that is and will ever be are at His command.

Without God I am:

Powerless, anticipating the impact of things I cannot control.

With God I am:

Empowered, with reverence for an Almighty God, honoring the Majesty of His awesome power.

Right Choices:

Let go of my will to serve me, and let His abiding love settle gently on my mind to empower me (see Joshua 4:24).

January 2 – God is Creator

The Bible says, "For since the creation of the world God's invisible qualities--his eternal power and divine nature--have been clearly seen, being understood from what has been made, so that men are without excuse" (Romans. 1:20).

Creator of all things and us, lasting and immortal.

Without God I am:

Creator of the things of my hands, given to dust.

With God I am:

Created daily in the likeness of God, redeemed and eternal.

Right Choices:

All that I am and all that I do to be right comes from Him, give thanks (see Isaiah 42:5).

January 3 – God is All-Knowing

The Bible says, "Great is our Lord and mighty in power; his understanding has no limit" (Psalms 147:5).

All Knowing, charting every day of the universe and our lives.

Without God I am:

Knowledgeable, my wisdom but foolishness to God.

With God I am:

Knowledgeable, about the things of God, His wisdom abiding.

Right Choices:

What is wisdom but knowing what is right with God, keep my pride in check (see John 18:4).

January 4 – God is Merciful

The Bible says, "The Lord is gracious and compassionate, slow to anger and rich in love" (Psalms 145:8).

Merciful, blessing us with only good things while allowing individual trials to strengthen our soul.

Without God I am:

Wretched, blind to the things of God, feeling victimized.

With God I am:

Blessed, with the richness of His mercy and grace, and abundant life, interrupted by pain and growth.

Right Choices:

Show kindness and mercy, you never know the path of another and the hurt experienced, be healing salve (see Genesis 19:16).

January 5 – God is Deliverer

The Bible says, "Yet I am poor and needy; come quickly to me, O God. You are my help and my deliverer; O Lord, do not delay" (Psalms 70:5).

Deliverer, came that we might live, sacrificing His life for our atonement, suffering at the hands of unbelief and prideful rage.

Without God, I am:

Unbelieving, I thirst and cry for His death in my life, my pride crucifies Him daily with rejection, yet He is all around me.

With God I am:

Believing, through faith and trust, I experience His healing touch on my life and know experientially that He is mine.

Right Choices:

Pass it on, build faith and trust with other people as the light of Christ illuminates from your soul (see 2 Samuel 22:2)

January 6 – God is Sinless

The Bible says, "For God made him who had no sin to be sin for us so that in him we might become the righteousness of God" (2 Corinthians 5:21).

Sinless, His standards and actions are excellent and perfect, in need of no improvement - only the best ever indeed!

Without God I am:

Godless, careless, and impulsive thinking causes grief and hasty actions, compromising ideals from muted whispers of conscience, driving secret acts and indifference to unloving deeds.

With God I am:

Mindful, bowing to the presence of God and recognizing the subtle compromises to lower standards, giving it all a good pre-tense and motive, while knowing the shame, my sin will bring.

Right Choices:

It all starts with each little victory, not in striving, but in surrendering (see 1 Peter 2:22).

January 7 – God is a Path Maker

The Bible says, "You have made known to me the path of life; you will fill me with joy in your presence, with eternal pleasures at your right hand" (Psalms 16:11).

Path Maker, with His loving guiding hand upon our lives, He is leading our heart onto a lighted path where He desires us to travel.

Without God I am:

A path finder, seeking a self-chosen path, frustrated and exhausted from wrong choices, rewarded with gratification, but empty.

With God I am:

A path follower, seeking His way, filled with His courage and patient endurance, knowing God is leading me where He wants me to be at journey's end, in His peace and satisfied.

Right Choices:

Take a hand today and guide another to a better place (see Ecclesiastes 11:5).

January 8 – God is Allowing Satan

The Bible says, "The Lord said to Satan, "Very well, then, everything he has is in your hands, but on the man, himself do not lay a finger." Then Satan went out from the presence of the Lord" (Job 1:12).

God is allowing Satan, to reign in this world as the deceiver, liar, cheater, and destroyer. Satan seeks only our total destruction and separation from God eternally, to be in Hell forever, a living torment.

Without God I am:

Lost, Satan has numbed my mind to the things of God, and evil spirits work to fill my life with good things, keeping me from want, caught in the snare of lustful passions.

With God I am:

Found, sensitive to my fallen ways, seeking higher ground and fighting the battle in my mind with remembrances of the risen self and who I am in Christ, banishing all evils of gloom - found.

Right Choices:

Would my Mom be proud of me, knowing I did this (see 1 Corinthians 10:13).

January 9 – God is Purposeful

The Bible says, "But the plans of the Lord stand firm forever, the purposes of his heart through all generations" (Psalms 33:11).

Purposeful, while this world is full of trouble and pain, God allows it in my life so that a precious secret will be found, bringing me now and in eternal life a crown of glory.

Without God I am:

Afflicted, caught in the frustration and failures that are hard to bear, I turn inward wandering to places that bring more significant trouble and sorrow to me and to others.

With God I am:

Seeking, to learn the purpose of life's trials and wanting a deeper understanding of His Glory meant for me now and forever.

Right Choices:

Think about what I'm doing; take it to the extremes, to where is it leading me at the end of the day? Today say to myself, I want to be intentional and not do what comes naturally (see 2 Corinthians 5:5).

January 10 – God is Glory

The Bible says, "In that day the Lord Almighty will be a glorious crown, a beautiful wreath for the remnant of his people" (Isaiah 28:5).

Glory, His creation displays splendor of Himself, shining
to the perfect day triumphant beauty radiance divine.

Without God I am:

Glorious, in what I have achieved and obtained, but my heart is guarded to things of God, pausing to enjoy "things" of creation, but viewing them as objects only to be used - enjoyed.

With God I am:

Glorious, in Christ, His Glory fills the skies, gladdens my eyes and re-assures my spirit, removing fear and doubt, His abiding presence gives me victory over my sinful ways.

Right Choices:

Yes, I'm one with the Lord, a chosen soul, partner with the Living King. My allegiance today is with Him – moment to moment (see Exodus 15:1).

January 11 – God is Renewal

The Bible says, "In reply Jesus declared, "I tell you the truth, no one can see the kingdom of God unless he is born again" (John 3:3).

Renewal, firm in His purpose, eyes filled with love and care, He looks at my condition with compassion and directs my heart to where He would have my life's purpose.

Without God I am:

Renewed, by the strength that comes from learning things and loving others, becoming assured and encouraged by all this and what it offers me, disappointment grows as relations fail.

With God I am:

Renewed, by the depth of His love for me, which strengthens my heart and adds courage to my ways to seek others and share this love, encouraging growth in becoming all God wants me to be.

Right Choices:

The renewal of my mind today begins with this time in His word, my new birth created from the womb of God, a miracle of Grace (see Titus 3:5).

January 12 – God is Shepherd

The Bible says, "For this is what the Sovereign Lord says; I myself will search for my sheep and look after them" (Ezekiel 34:11).

Shepherd, His goodness, and love are a shield to my life, His mercy and care extend to those who love Him, pardoning all sin and sparing sorrow.

Without God I am:

A lost sheep, prone to seek the path I choose, seeking the comfort of other lost sheep, feeling assurance in numbers. The direction is in vain and leads to despair; sorrow comes to its rightful owner.

With God I am:

His sheep, prone to wander from His path, He inclines a gracious ear to hear my prayer, my works cannot win His favor, only my humble repentant heart, trusting His loving ways, not mine.

Right Choices:

Let the Lord's eyes fall on me today and find me leading a lost soul (see 1 Peter 5:2).

January 13 – God was Crucified

The Bible says, "What shall I do, then, with Jesus who is called Christ?" Pilate asked. They all answered, "Crucify him!" Why? What crime has he committed?" asked Pilate. But they shouted all the louder, "Crucify him" (Matthew 27:22,23).

Crucified, killed by the hateful pride and anxious hearts, men fearful of the God-Man who healed the sick- Jesus Christ came as God's Son, His -perfect sinless sacrifice poured out for His chosen ones.

Without God I am:

Condemned, God loves saint and sinner alike, he came not to condemn the world, but to save the world from sin and it's destructive nature - choose Him as He has chosen you.

With God I am:

Redeemed, by the blood of the Lamb, the perfect sacrifice for my sins - when God looks at me, He sees my redemptive self - washed white as snow, seeing Jesus within me, a living sacrifice.

Right Choices:
Time to nail my destructive patterns to the cross of Christ (see 1Peter 2:24).

January 14 – God is a Fortress

The Bible says, "The Lord is my rock, my fortress, and my deliverer; my God is my rock, in whom I take refuge, He is my shield and the horn of my salvation, my stronghold" (Psalms 18:2).

Fortress, a refuge of strength, power, and might - He is among us providing all that He is to all that we need to be.

Without God I am:

Ruins, the crumbled remains of a mighty life of efforts lay in utter destruction, a trembling deserted heart looks on at vengeful evil enemies who will violate all that I am and hope to be till I despair.

With God I am:

Temple, desiring to be pleasing to God, I fill my body with the good things of God, honoring Him and praising who He is and what He has done for me, my protector, shield, and fortress.

Right Choices:
I may think I'm standing alone fighting this all by myself, but if only I could see the legions of God's warriors by my side – fight the fight (see Psalm 144:2).

January 15 – God is Light

The Bible says, "He reveals deep and hidden things; he knows what lies in darkness, and light dwells with him" (Daniel 2:22).

Light, God lightens my soul with His presence like the night, giving way to a bright new day.

Without God I am:

Darkness, driven by evil spirits day and night, my very existence is threatened by the toils upon my body and life.

With God I am:

Lighted, turning from the dark to the light, I see the brightness of His glorious face on my soul, extending Himself now onto my heart.

Right Choices:

Today, stand in the light, which means the path is known and the way leads to a right place, rest in His peace (see 2 Corinthians 4:4).

JANUARY 16 – GOD IS RULER

The Bible says, "But be sure to fear the Lord and serve him faithfully with all your heart; consider what great things he has done for you" (1 Samuel 12:24).

Ruler, He holds the universe in place, commands the boundaries of the oceans and yet He lets me make the choice to rule my life or join in fellowship with Him as His disciple.

Without God I am:

Independent, knowing the way I want to go and the choices that make sense to me, I push on toward results, getting and going somewhere but nowhere in the end.

With God I am:

Dependent, even if prone to rule my own way. But, I know a God who is the ruler of all, able to create in the hearts of man a decision that favors His way - it seems self-serving, but obedience lies at its root.

Right Choices:

Where is this temptation coming from, and who is demanding my allegiance? Take heed and serve the true Master, the Lord (see Ezekiel 28:2).

January 17 – God is Freedom

The Bible says, "Now the Lord is the Spirit, and where the Spirit of the Lord is, there is freedom" (2 Corinthians 3:17).

Freedom, His space, and boundaries are endless yet strict, large enough to allow an incredible journey of a lifetime, the path being narrow, yet beautiful, challenging and rewarding.

Without God I am:

Bound by, the world's demands and driven to fill my empty heart, I feel gratified but not satisfied, the only answer is more, more, and more.

With God I am:

Free, to be the person God intended, resting in the completeness of Christ, I heartily claim the greatness of God to fill my incompleteness.

Right Choices:

Freedom in the oneness of my surrender to the Holy Spirit; knowing that whatever I do in this state is perfect and totally acceptable to my Lord, Jesus Christ (see Galatians 5:1).

January 18 – God is a Sanctuary

The Bible says, "The heavens praise your wonders, O Lord, your faithfulness too, in the assembly of the holy ones" (Psalms 89:5).

Sanctuary, where the souls of the Christians delight in singing praises to Him and worshipping His Majesty, growing in the knowledge of God.

Without God I am:

A mere occupant of a church, a building like any other place where I come to be seen, not to hear God or to be heard by Him.

With God I am:

A part of the church, joining with friends to meet God, to share His love, casting all our cares on a loving God in praise and worship, learning, growing, and desiring to make Him known to others.

Right Choices:

Be intentional today about where I go, with my mind and my body. The sacredness of His presence is holy ground (see Hebrews 9:1-10).

January 19 – God is Father

The Bible says, "Every good and perfect gift is from above, coming down from the Father of the heavenly lights, who does not change like shifting shadows. He chose to give us birth through the word of truth, that we might be a kind of firstfruits of all he created" (James 1:17-18).

Father, Holy, and perfect He seeks to restore and mend where earthly parents failed, His love, care, and nurture seek to heal my inner soul.

Without God I am:

Orphaned, cast from generation to generation, I live with undeserving afflictions from parents who in their sin failed in so many ways - my hurt is lasting.

With God I am:

Adopted, by my Heavenly Father, my life is taking on new meaning as I listen to Him and what He wants me to do and be. His enabling hand is directing and guiding my every step.

Right Choices:

Be the father of a friend today that, they may never have had, caring and showing understanding and encouragement (see 2 Corinthians 6:18).

January 20 – God is Impartial

The Bible says, "But the wisdom that comes from heaven is first of all pure; then peace-loving, considerate, submissive, full of mercy and good fruit, impartial and sincere" (James 3:17).

Impartial, He loves all His children equally, His measure not in what we have, but who we are and wanting all to have all of whom He is now and forever.

Without God I am:

Partial, sharp distinct lines divide my life for what I love and dislike, the value established by worldly standards and the passion of the day and how it feeds me.

With God I am:

Partial, desiring the things of God, challenged by my world around me to get in step, but choosing the rhythm of a simpler way, blessed assurance, Jesus is mine.

Right Choices:

Look at this person and/or my situation today with "newness" and a perspective that is fresh, free from baggage and bondage (see James 3:17).

January 21 – God is Healer

The Bible says. "…who forgives all your sins and heals all your diseases, who redeems your life from the pit and crowns you with love and compassion, who satisfies your desires with good things so that your youth is renewed like the eagles" (Psalms 103: 3-5).

Healer, God touches the blind man and he sees. He makes the lame walk; He dies on a cross and enables the sinner
to become a saint.

Without God I am:

Hurt, afflicted and injured my body heals, but my heart
longs and aches for true healing.

With God I am:

Healed, held in the grip of infinite Love, my longings embrace a God who will never lose hold of me. His Spirit is at work within me, drawing me to Him and others.

Right Choices:

Be the healing portion in someone's life today by taking action to bless another's life with a portion of my bountifulness (see Psalm 147:1).

January 22 – God is Rest

The Bible says, "Come to me, all you who are weary and burdened, and I will give you rest" (Matthew 11:28).

Rest, His gracious presence and assurance calms the air, quiets the raging sea, stills time for a moment to draw strength from I am, that I am.

Without God I am:

Restless, from where do I come and to where do I go? Will this happen to me, and how will I manage? My life is filled with questions.

With God I am:

Restful, knowing Jesus will sustain me, and help me. His grace is at work deep within my soul preserving me with a newness of life and strength.

Right Choices:

Rest in the assurance of God Almighty's hand on my life, preserving, protecting, and providing the strength and courage to endure and work through whatever is placed on the path of my life (see Proverbs 24:33).

January 23 – God is Unchanging

The Bible says, "Your faithfulness continues through all generations, you established the earth, and it endures" (Psalms 119:90).

Unchanging, from centuries that have gone to those that shall be, God is the same yesterday, today and forever.

Without God I am:

Changing, becoming more of what I would have myself be, fearful of change, but not wanting another year like the one that just pasted.

With God I am:

Changing, becoming more like Jesus each day, yet failing with innumerable mistakes, I press onto a future which may seem scary at times. I'm content to be going His way.

Right Choices:

Listen to the drum beat of my weary ways with a new "alertness" and desire to change. Let the only change be for me to become more like Jesus (see Hebrews 6:17).

January 24 – God is Successful

The Bible says, "But the eyes of the Lord are on those who fear him, on those whose hope is in his unfailing love, to deliver them from death and keep them alive in famine" (Psalms 33:18-19).

Successful, God uses all things to His Glory, His plans are perfect and happen in His time with triumphant results.

Without God I am:

Pursuing, setting goals and charting my path, I fail my way to the kind of success, the world loudly applauds, but I'm not sure I am climbing the right ladder.

With God I am:

Successful, used by God, going forward with a real sense of forgiveness, trust, mercy, and power to use my regretted mistakes and forgiven sins as a qualification to help others.

Right Choices:

Success has many flavors, look not only at the things achieved but areas where I steered clear and prevented mistakes and failures, all with a thankful heart (see Joshua 1:8).

January 25 – God is Friend

The Bible says, "When Jesus saw their faith, he said, "Friend, your sins are forgiven. Luke 5:20 You are my friends if you do what I command" (John 15:14).

Friend, dwelling within every human heart, He waits to be known when His whispers finally enter a deaf ear, daily counsel creates assurance - He wants the best and will deliver His all.

Without God I am:

Foe, foreign to His divine plan and blessings are given, My life seeks relations that prosper me, liking the way I feel when around that person, I seek them out.

With God I am:

Friendly, lighted with His overflowing presence, my heart reaches out to others with un-weighted care, my only storm the passion I have for sharing Him.

Right Choices:

To have a friend is to be a friend, but often I need to let another know about my needs – be a fueler, while letting others fuel me (see - John 15:13).

January 26 – God is Forgiver

The Bible says, "You are forgiving and good, O Lord, abounding in love to all who call to you" (Psalms 86:5).

Forgiver, knowing the shortness of our days, His compassion reigns supreme, granting true forgiveness for our sins, through our Faith in His Son, our Spirits bound for Glory.

Without God I am:

Burdened, by the guilt and shame of lost innocence, I know not where relief will come from, my soul, condemned to pay the price, I gave not to Jesus, the redeemer for all - lost.

With God I am:

Forgiven, while pledged to Jesus, my life's actions have so often denied that which my lips have said, creed and conduct not the same, my sins put at Calvary's cross, strengthened by the loss.

Right Choices:

This is huge! Yes, I remember my transgressions in life, but it is time to move on and not think myself bigger than God. Today, I need to forgive myself as God has with true confession and pardon – I am free (see Ephesians 4:32).

January 27 – God is Serenity

The Bible says, "Peace I leave with you; my peace I give you. I do not give to you as the world gives. Do not let your hearts be troubled and do not be afraid" (John 14:27).

Serenity, He is quieting the troubled mind, guiding and directing us to His purpose and plan, guiding our will onto His way, defeating evil, disease, and pain.

Without God I am:

Troubled, desiring not to submit or cooperate with Him, defeating Him by choice and allowing self to go another way, my life has no ultimate good but the things I gave away.

With God I am:

Affirmed, by my readiness to submit to Him and to cooperate, knowing God is weaving my troubled past into a quiet purpose and pattern of ultimate good, I press on daily.

Right Choices:

When I look at who I am, I see the perfect reflection of a saved sinful saint – born again by the redemptive blood of Christ (see Micah 6:8).

January 28 – God is Master

The Bible says, "The disciples went and woke him, saying, "Master, Master, we're going to drown!" He got up and rebuked the wind and the raging waters; the storm subsided, and all was calm" (Luke 8:24).

Master, at time's end, may all that we've seen over the vastness of years, be the splendor, radiance, and care of His love over the lives of human hearts and souls.

Without God I am:

Master, of my own destiny, my legacy stands in the splendor of achievements, wealth gained, and lives touched, distinguished for me today, but the glow fades quickly as I seek more significant things.

With God I am:

Mastered, by the Hand of God, obscure, unassuming, and humbled, I praise a glorious God that at days end, is illuminated in my life - pointing the way unto Him and my life eternal with Him in Heaven.

Right Choices:

Serve today, the Master who wants to build me, not destroy me (see Luke 20:21).

January 29 – God is Immense

The Bible says, "Where were you when I laid the earth's foundation? Tell me, if you understand" (Job 38:4).

Immense, a tornado cannot move Him, the ocean cannot cover Him, all the winds cannot bend Him, the universe cannot contain Him, yet He lives in hearts, complete and whole.

Without God I am:

Finite, in power and strength to become what really matters, the person God wants me to be, my creator and companion.

With God I am:

Infinite, in power and strength to overcome the forces of evil, letting an awesome abiding God clean my heart and enable me on His path.

Right Choices:

My perspective today of the importance of my life rests on the assurance that God died for me as if I were the only one that mattered. However, I'm equal to the billions who share this amazing gift and of no greater importance, go in humbleness (see 1Timothy 1:16).

January 30 – God is Rich

The Bible says, "Whoever trusts in his riches will fall, but the righteous will thrive like a green leaf" (Proverbs 11:28).

Rich, He owns it all, created it all, for all mankind,
it simply all belongs to Him, He wants us to use it wisely.

Without God I am:

Materialistic, coveting the things others have, I want and drive my life and those around me to seek and own more "things", thinking all goodness is on its way to me.

With God I am:

Steward, taking care of each thing God has gifted to me, I praise Him in thanksgiving, desiring to share with those in need, my blessings becoming a blessing to others.

Right Choices:

My richness today and forever is not in what I have, but in who I am, in Christ (see Isaiah 45:3).

January 31 – God is a Shield

The Bible says, "For surely, O LORD, you bless the righteous; you surround them with your favor as with a shield" (Psalms 5:12).

Shield, He protects and sustains those who call Him - Lord.

Without God I am:

Vulnerable, to the perils of life and the enemy within.

With God I am:

Protected, by a loving God who wants only what is best for me.

Right Choices:

Standing today in the shadow of God Almighty fearing to go to any place where my thoughts or body would be where God is not (see 2 Samuel 22:31).

February 1 – God is Strength

The Bible says, "The LORD is my strength and my song; he has become my salvation. He is my God, and I will praise him, my father's God, and I will exalt him" (Exodus 15:2).
Strength, of my life, whom or what shall I fear?
Without God I am:

Weak, relying on my knowledge, wisdom, and ability to discipline my life, I seek success on an endless path
of discontentment.

With God I am:

Strengthened, by a redeeming God who is incredible in
every nature, He enables me to do His will.

Right Choices:

When I am weak, than I am strong, says the Lord, for my strength comes from God alone (see Isaiah 49:5).

February 2 – God is Risen

The Bible says, "Then go quickly and tell his disciples: `He has risen from the dead and is going ahead of you into Galilee. There you will see him.' Now I have told you" (Mathew 28:7).

Risen, from the dead, in payment for all my sins, He lives now and forever.

Without God I am:

Fallen, to a lower natural nature that seeks to place our unholy selves as god over our lives.

With God I am:

Saved, from eternal damnation and entrusted to a God who is redeeming my life daily, through the sanctification of an obedient will.

Right Choices:

Rise with Him, in my thinking today, in what I do and all I think (see 1 Cor. 15:14).

February 3 – God is Disciplined

The Bible says, "Through him and for his name's sake, we received grace and apostleship to call people from among all the Gentiles to the obedience that comes from faith" (Romans 1:5).

Disciplined, order, organization and strict, unbending laws govern the universe, the right and wrong of His way, the black and white have no gray.

Without God I am:

Ungoverned, prone to choose which rules apply, my choices for today seem best for short term gain for me.

With God I am:

Governed, by a God I love, I chose to let Him be my conscience, desiring daily to do and be action-oriented in my life towards serving Him.

Right Choices:

What is discipline but doing what is best for me anyway, so get on with it now (see Proverbs 13:24).

February 4 – God is Worthy

The Bible says, "Great is the LORD and most worthy of praise; his greatness no one can fathom" (Psalm 145:3).

Worthy, the supreme manifestation of all that is good, right and Glorious.

Without God I am:

Unworthy, God loves the saint and sinner alike, He came to redeem each lost soul, precious in His sight, but without Him eternally in our lives, we are worthless at days end.

With God I am:

Wealthy, God has taken an unworthy soul and granted a gift that could not be purchased, but its value is greater than gold - peace, joy, salvation, loving, caring and serving.

Right Choices:

Worthy is the Lamb, he paid it all and all to him I owe, dwell on this today (see Philippians 4:8).

February 5 – God is Forever

The Bible says, "I am the Alpha and the Omega," says the Lord God, "who is, and who was, and who is to come, the Almighty" (Revelation 1:8).

Forever, He is the Alpha and the Omega, always was and always will be, no human mind can grasp the meaning of such as this.

Without God I am:

Forever Lost, life on earth is but a brief period in time, compared to the eternity of my existence in Hell, separated from God, forever lost and damned.

With God I am:

Forever Found, living each day in a renewed sense, I realize and enjoy the importance of each day and who I am for Him, building glory for a longer stay in a better place prepared for me.

Right Choices:

We will never die when thinking of the short term gain a sin may bring, think more about an internal blessing lost forever (see Exodus 15:18).

February 6 – God is Living

The Bible says, "My soul yearns, even faints, for the courts of the LORD; my heart and my flesh cry out for the living God" (Psalm 84:2).

Living, a force beyond human conception, this God is Big, not distant but near to each heart, He claims as His.

Without God I am:

Dying, my mind and body are in decay, a short span-of-time that will yield bones to dust and soul to eternal despair.

With God I am:

Alive, in Christ, He searches the innermost part of who I am, and seeks to guide and direct me unto higher ground daily, restoring my lost self to eternal glory.

Right Choices:

When you begin to feel you are all so alone, that God is distant and not near or caring, think about the God who says he will never leave you or forsake you (see Hebrews 13:5).

February 7 – God is Teacher

The Bible says, "Call to me and I will answer you and tell you great and unsearchable things you do not know" (Jeremiah 33:3).

Teacher, He wants our minds to understand, our hearts to feel and our lives to touch, complicated but simple. Let chaos, doubt, strife, and fear be comforted by Him to bring calm, assurance and peace.

Without God I am:

Taught, when hated to hate, when injured to pass judgment, when in doubt to fear, when despaired to tremble, when filled with darkness to see gloom, when sad to feel only heartfelt pain.

With God I am:

Taught, when hated to love, when injured to pardon, when doubtful to have faith, when despaired to have hope, when dark I seek His word, when saddened to draw near to Him and be filled with joy.

Right Choices:

Ask now what is troubling your mind, let God's amazing grace enter and soothe your soul (see Job 36:22).

February 8 – God is Righteous

The Bible says, "but let him who boasts boast about this: that he understands and knows me, that I am the LORD, who exercises kindness, justice and righteousness on earth, for in these I delight, declares the LORD" (Jeremiah 9:24).

Righteous, magnificent in all that He is, now and forever, His divine nature is truly holy in every imaginable definition.

Without God I am:

Rebellious, willful acts of disobedience fill my life as I seek to serve myself as god-man - unholy.
With God I am:

Virtuous, moral and seeking to be Godlike in all that I think – say and do, wanting to be just and right in all my dealings.
Right Choices:

The holiness of God has no place with the stench of my sin, smell me for who I really am and be deodorized with the saving Grace of Christ today, pray for healing now (see 2 Samuel 22:21).

FEBRUARY 9 – GOD IS JUDGE

The Bible says, "Since you call on a Father who judges each man's work impartially, live your lives as strangers here in reverent fear" (1Peter 1:17).

Judge, every knee shall bow, and tongue confess, that Jesus Christ is Lord. He reigns as the ultimate authority over all, coming one day to judge the quick and the dead.

Without God I am:

Judged, condemned by my reluctance to seek Jesus and be redeemed by His blood, Jesus' death for my sins, the only way to salvation and life eternal in heaven.

With God I am:

Justified, by Christ and what He did for me, what God sees when He looks at me is Christ Jesus and my redeemed self.

Right Choices:

Recognize the areas of my life today that need work and be open to letting God do His work, this is about Him, not me doing the doing (see - Deuteronomy 31:6).

February 10 – God is Divine

The Bible says, "For since the creation of the world God's invisible qualities--his eternal power and divine nature--have been clearly seen, being understood from what has been made, so that men are without excuse" (Romans 1:20).

Divine, solemn wondrous spangled heavens proclaim
and display the Creators mighty hand, no voice or sound
is heard, but we look and see all is truly - divine.

Without God I am:

Diva, on the stage of life, my prima donna attitude creates an awe of admiration from those empowering me.

With God I am:

Divinely, enabled by a Supreme and Sacred God, my life and God-given power proclaims the Majesty of a Mighty God who is now and forever to be praised in thanksgiving.

Right Choices:

Look at people and "things" the way God does, not with my sinful bent and lustful slant, take higher ground and perspective today (see 2Peter 1:3).

February 11 – God is Authority

The Bible says, "For our struggle is not against flesh and blood, but against the rulers, against the authorities, against the powers of this dark world and against the spiritual forces of evil in the heavenly realms" (Ephesians 6:12).

Authority, who or what can challenge His ultimate essence,
He is that He is, yet our mortal soul stands in self-defiance,
proclaiming I am. God's patience with such denial will end.

Without God I am:

Authored, by the created laws and ways of man, I seek a balanced life believing a chosen path alone from God will lead me well; I'm as good as the next guy, maybe a bit better - all is well.

With God I am:

Authenticated, by a loving God and indwelling Spirit, I travel a higher moral road, given to be sidetracked, the Lord guides me back, like a child who wanders dangerously from a parent's track.

Right Choices:

Freedom to choose for me today means something new; it's not just about me, but also my Lord and Savior (see Romans 13:1).

February 12 – God is Redeemer

The Bible says, "In him we have redemption through his blood, the forgiveness of sins, in accordance with the riches of God's grace" (Ephesians 1:7).

Redeemer, broken and bleeding a cruel death for our sins, but death could not hold Him, unconquered by death and Hell, where He left our pardoned guilt - every man by His Love to be free.

Without God I am:

Reckoned, to a fate of daily choices, that weighs on the heart and produces complacent joy, at day's end the best that I was, not enough to pay the penalty of all my sins.

With God I am:

Rescued, daily to make better choices, I seek relations with a Lord who knows what is best, His promises revealed in His Word.

Right Choices:

Yes, Christ died once for all to pay a price for my salvation that only Christ could pay, but now, my choice to partake is given by God daily, chose well my friend, and be blessed (see - Isaiah 54:5).

February 13 – God is Faithful

The Bible says, "Righteousness will be his belt and faithfulness the sash around his waist. Isaiah 11:5

Faithful, as sure as the day is new, as repeatable as tides
flowing twice daily; it is our trusting belief and reliance on a God
of love and care.

Without God I am:

Faithless, prone to a duty that is self-serving, allegiances
formed out of depravity, a treacherous path I seek.

With God I am:

Faithful, confiding in the Lord who reigns in my life,
I feel His ever-presence drawing near, my purpose
now ever more clear.

Right Choices:

While it all seems so easy and straight forward, the battle to be faithful is huge, with one exception. In Christ we are free, so dwell deeply and richly in Him today and let his grace abound (see 1Corinthians 10:13).

February 14 – God is Holy

The Bible says, "It is because of him that you are in Christ Jesus, who has become for us wisdom from God--that is, our righteousness, holiness and redemption" (1 Corinthians 1:30).

Holy, only God is untainted with the stains of sin. No temptation overtook Him, only right - no wrong distinguished as marrow to bone, white from black- He's leading us Home.

Without God I am:

Profane, foolish in my proclamations of who I am and what I do, my ever-present evil is a stench unto an unseen Holy God, His cleansing power is at hand, wanting to deodorize me.

With God I am:

Consecrated, with the God I love, a boundless sense of devotion invades a dedicated heart.

Right Choices:

How can it be, this mortal body stained but washed as white as snow, clean forevermore? Stay on the highway, don't get in the mud, stay in the vine, divine (see Psalm 99:9).

February 15 – God is Presence

The Bible says, "The LORD himself goes before you and will be with you; he will never leave you nor forsake you. Do not be afraid; do not be discouraged" (Deuteronomy 31:8).

Presence, wherever we go, there we are, but also there is God, upholding us with His power, safe and assured.

Without God I am:

Possessive, while aware of God, He is distant to me, I pursue the things of this world, desiring each to fill
my empty self.

With God I am:

Possessed, by the authentic nature of God to the point
where for me, the important "I" stands surrendered, filling me with His Love.

Right Choices:

Look in the mirror today and see not only the reflection of me, but a God indwelling who cares and is as close to me as the fragrance that dwells on a rose (see Jude 1:24).

February 16 – God is Free

The Bible says, "The Spirit and the bride say, "Come!" And let him who hears say, "Come!" Whoever is thirsty, let him come; and whoever wishes, let him take the free gift of the water of life" (Revelation 22:17).

Free, He gave His Life, a Gift for me, priceless in value, precious and dear, divinely to be mine for all time.

Without God I am:

Valued, God wants to own this heart. He died for all sinners alike, pause now your hurried path and look upon a God, who cares so much for you, desiring none would be lost.

With God I am:

Valuable, in who God is and what He's making of me, Christ's Love and Glory is overflowing through me - to others.

Right Choices:

Free to be, but oh, the price that He paid! How can this be so valuable, but yet "free"? It is not easy to see, but look today and "think" about the price paid to set me free (see Romans 5:17).

February 17 – God is Peace

The Bible says, "And the peace of God, which transcends all understanding, will guard your hearts and your minds in Christ Jesus" (Philippians 4:7).

Peace, God quiets the soul, calms the disturbances of life
to add harmony, order, and freedom from strife, Godly medicine to the soul of man.

Without God I am:

Tentative, my peace comes from a state of being, owning, or going and coming from places and things of value,
all is well as long as well is good.

With God I am:

Peaceful, mindful of who God is and His Love for me,
assurance is mine through a Jesus Divine.

Right Choices:

This tender morsel from God is so unnoticed and under- appreciated, like a warm coat; it comforts us beyond our understanding and care; be thankful for this precious gift (see Isaiah 54:10).

February 18 – God is Righteous

The Bible says, "As for God, his way is perfect; the word of the LORD is flawless. He is a shield for all who take refuge in him" (Psalm 18:30).

Righteous, ultimate virtue in all that He does, His essence can do no wrong, for only what is right, what is admirable and what is correct is part of God's plan.

Without God I am:

Rightful, claiming my portion for what I seek, it may be good it may be bad for what I keep.

With God I am:

Right, always on the correct side, standing with Him in watchful care, my beloved Master shares.

Right Choices:

Right choices always seem to be unrealistic, and they are, given my sinful nature. Choose today whom you serve, and think about who I am in Christ (see Psalms 7:9).

February 19 – God is Alpha & Omega

The Bible says, "I am the Alpha and the Omega," says the Lord God, "who is, and who was, and who is to come, the Almighty" (Revelation 1:8).

Alpha and Omega, the first and the last, the beginning and the end, which was and which is to come, forever till time should ever end.

Without God I am:

Temporal, at my life's end I see now a God who called for me daily, screaming in terror at my loss, the tears from His face, desiring that none would be lost.

With God I am:

Temporal, in this life which is but a speck of time, to be re-united with the God I love, but who loves me beyond understanding, now and forever.

Right Choices:

God started it all and is going to end it all. My ending means everything because the product will be my legacy. Let the building blocks of today become a monument to God (see Proverbs 3:35).

FEBRUARY 20 – GOD IS ALMIGHTY

The Bible says, "He who forms the mountains, creates the wind, and reveals his thoughts to man, he who turns dawn to darkness, and treads the high places of the earth-- the LORD God Almighty is his name" (Amos 4:13).

Almighty, who can understand the might of anything that is, was and will ever be, creator not created, the Source of all that is, I am that I am, His plan unstoppable except by my willful choice for me.

Without God I am:

Mightily, engaged in life to create and be everything that I can be, gifted with talent from God, His plan was perfect but I had better thoughts.

With God I am:

Mightily, engaged in life to create and be everything that God wants me to be, His plan perfect, and while I stray off the path, His light in my heart guides me back - thank you Jesus!

Right Choices:

Almighty, one with Him! May I stand in the shadow of his grace today and be blessed (see Jeremiah 13:16).

FEBRUARY 21 – GOD IS LORD

The Bible says, "You know the message God sent to the people of Israel, telling the good news of peace through Jesus Christ, who is Lord of all" (Acts 10:36).

Lord, one with God, Holy incarnate Jesus Christ, one with the Holy Spirit given for all, to be saved from the wages of sin, death eternally separated from God - but no! - united with Him!!

Without God I am:

Lord, of my life and permitted by God to choose, allowed to be free in sinfulness, a power that feels so good, so open to be what I see, Satan deceives me.

With God I am:

Lordship, seeks to reign in place of self-will, desiring to be Christ-like, I put Him over my will, my mind and ask that He guide me in what I do, peaceful and content I serve others too.

Right Choices:

Lord, such a small word, cherish it today and let Him speak to you, where you are, let Him take you now to higher ground. The power in this four-letter word is awesome (see Zechariah 6:15).

February 22 – God is Rejoicing

The Bible says, "I tell you that in the same way there will be more rejoicing in heaven over one sinner who repents than over ninety-nine righteous persons who do not need to repent" (Luke 15:7).

Rejoicing, when one who was lost is found, when we say "yes" to Him and "no" to sin, when at days end, we meet - well done my good and faithful servant, come and enjoy your reward.

Without God I am:

Rejoicing, when fulfilled with the pursuit of a hard-won battle, joy-filled in the presence of the moment, happy and
thankful to be who I am - for now.

With God I am:

Rejoicing, for now in my victories, knowing my strength comes from the Lord, truly heightened to the realm of a Divine experience, I praise God for who I am in Him.

Right Choices:

Envision the gates of heaven with the thousand cheering voices of friends of the past, waving you on to the finish line as you face your choice of righteousness today (see Psalm 19:8).

February 23 – God is Protection

The Bible says, "For he will command his angels concerning you to guard you in all your ways;" (Psalm 91:11).

Protection, from evils that seek my utter destruction with disease and mental ruin, His Angels stand on guard to do my battle.

Without God I am:

Exposed, to the rages of sin, which retreat when evil knows that victory is sure, "let this soul alone," they say for he/she is mine.

With God I am:

Pursued, by evil thoughts from enemy spirits, daily skirmishes lost to evil, and also at times, a major battle lost. I approach the Cross and offer my brokenness for His wholeness.

Right Choices:

Would you go out to kill a bear with a slingshot, only if you were drunk? Don't be drunk on your pride; Satan is thousand times smarter than you or I, carry the big gun, who goes by the name of the Son (see Psalm 5:11).

February 24 – God is Justice

The Bible says – Since you call on a Father who judges each man's work impartially, live your lives as strangers here in reverent fear" (1Peter 1:17).

Justice, giving to each what is due and rewarding those who live for Him and His purpose and plan.

Without God I am:

Justified, by my comparison to the ways of man, my "gold standard" is to do unto others before they do unto me.

With God I am:

Justified, by my Heavenly Father who carried all my sins to the Cross, sins of past, sins of today, and my sins forever - given not to a free will to sin, but repentant to a forgiving God.

Right Choices:

How does God look at everyone with no prejudice? I can't imagine, I'm prejudiced against myself. I know how bad I can be. Give someone a break today – the benefit of the doubt, they most likely really need it (see Psalm 94:15).

February 25 – God is Salvation

The Bible says, "Surely God is my salvation; I will trust and not be afraid. The LORD, the LORD, is my strength and my song; he has become my salvation" (Isaiah 12:2).

Salvation, saved "from what?," our mind asks, and if it only knew, a moment spent in Heaven or Hell would cause our mind, heart, and soul to fear, but yearn to be Saved.

Without God I am:

Lost, for eternal damnation and separation from God, forever in agony and despair beyond description.

With God I am:

Saved, once acclaimed never to be lost, finding glory,
building confidence and courage gained as my choices today lead me happily home - forever praising Him.

Right Choices:

Don't be saved for the moment of sin, a brief ecstasy, and indulgence into a dark space that feeds my lustful senses. Yes, good for the moment, but another moment is coming, and it is just around the corner, a short way down the road, getting nearer and nearer, let it be the right moment for you today. Think about what and whom you are feeding (see Isaiah 17:10)?

February 26 – God is Comforter

The Bible says, "Praise be to the God and Father of our Lord Jesus Christ, the Father of compassion and the God of all comfort" (2 Corinthians 1:3).

Comforter, the Lord is good, ready to clean a burdened heart and renew a right spirit within all believers.

Without God I am:

Un-confessed, His Almighty Goodness seeks this burdened heart and yearns to set it free and call it home to dwell with me, My overindulgence aims to fill a void that only He can fill.

With God I am:

Comforted, hurt, anxiety and daily wrongs afflict my spirit; burdens my soul, but these confessed and pardoned sins done against His Spirit are forgiven, and my heart is set free.

Right Choices:

See how many times you can say, thank you, Jesus today. That small voice is talking and telling you things, things that matter, and that help. Guiding you to a better place for sure – Thank you, Jesus (see Colossians 3:16)!

February 27 – God is Life

The Bible says, "For the wages of sin is death, but the gift of God is eternal life in Christ Jesus our Lord" (Romans 6:23).

Life, to all who are dead in Heart, He brings renewal, a Living God full of care and compassion, with believers every step of the way.

Without God I am:

Sick, all is not well with my soul, my soul longs for the Master's healing touch, all too long this soul has been starved from the things of God - its Maker and Redeemer.

With God I am:

Living, in the knowledge of Christ, His indwelling nature alive in me, empowering me to be a light among the lost, so that God the Author and Finisher of our Faith be Glorified.

Right Choices:

You know that what you may be thinking about yourself today doesn't matter. What matters is what you think God feels about you. You need to know today that this God thinks you are pretty amazing- listen to Him speak to your heart (see Psalms 23:6)!

February 28 – God is Protector

The Bible says, "The LORD will keep you from all harm-- he will watch over your life; 8the LORD will watch over your coming and going both now and forevermore" (Psalms 121:7-8).

Protector, His Angels stand guard all around believers, keeping them from unknown dangers and guiding them along a narrow worthy path.

Without God I am:

Exposed, misled by forces I do not understand, naked and hungry my will grabs most any hand, the path seems right to me, oh how good it feels to be free to do my will.

With God I am:

Protected, from not becoming the monster within, from not needing to suffer the consequences of sins not acted out or passions bred, I thank the Lord for what I have not become.

Right Choices:

I wonder if one day we'll meet the angels that stood watch over our wayward lives and hear their stories of what would have been, how they helped and see the twinkle in their eye and hear the laughter – believe it is so (see Luke 4:10).

February 29 – God is Love

The Bible says "Whoever does not love does not know God, because God is love" (1 John 4:8).

Love, He knit me together in my mother's womb, planning each day, giving my heart to be free to choose, knowing the errors of my ways, He planned a Redeemer to lighten my days.

Without God I am:

Loving, caring for those close to me, ones that matter most, I pick and choose the "right" ones deserving me - the host.

With God I am:

Loved, by a Heavenly Father, His love overflows from me to others, people of His choosing not mine, my spirit one with His, my life compassionate and truly divine.

Right Choices:

Like a mother's love, but stronger, embracing as a long lost friend greeting hug, soft and gentle eyes that look deeply into the soul and with the smile of a loving partner, saying – I love you. Think about Him this way today (see Psalms 36:7).

MARCH 1– GOD IS ADEQUACY

The Bible says, "For in Christ all the fullness of the Deity lives in bodily form, and you have been given fullness in Christ, who is the head over every power and authority" (Colossians 2:9,10).

Adequacy, in Him we are complete and lacking nothing,
His mercy and provision are ever-present and real.

Without God I am:

Addicted to my pursuit of worldly passions, I have little rest but yearn to be blest. If there is a God, where can He be? Oh, how I long to be set free.

With God I am:

Adequate, though my health may fail me, my job escapes me, comforts are gone, storms and trials abound, I will
rejoice in the Lord - my strength.

Right Choices:

Don't doubt this is true today! You may be feeling a 1,000 miles away from this at the moment, but listen, God gives just a little bit when the flour in the jar is almost gone, the bread to feed the five thousand starts with a few loaves – let Him give to you today, it will be what you need, perhaps not what you want (see Ephesians 3:19).

March 2 – God is Determined

The Bible says, "What do you think? If a man owns a hundred sheep, and one of them wanders away, will he not leave the ninety-nine on the hills and go to look for the one that wandered off? And if he finds it, I tell you the truth, he is happier about that one sheep than about the ninety-nine that did not wander off. In the same way your Father in heaven is not willing that any of these little ones should be lost" (Mathew 18:12-14).

Determined, that none would be lost; His patience and enduring love awaits our response, come now He beckons - before it is too late.

Without God I am:

Defiant, raising my rebellious nature against the things of God, my platitudes and excuses soothe my mind, but my soul longs for God.

With God I am:

Delivered, from the evils that lurk within, my heart, my mind, and soul are Spirit-filled with heavenly song.

Right Choices:

Be glad that He is, if He weren't, we all would be lost (see Isaiah 37:26).

March 3 – God is Awesome

The Bible says, "For the LORD your God is God of gods and Lord of lords, the great God, mighty and awesome, who shows no partiality and accepts no bribes" (Deuteronomy 10:17).

Awesome, what is it that eyes see, hearts feel and souls
rejoice in that is so amazing - a God who is so immense, wonderful, and divine - yet mine.

Without God I am:

Awful, extremely regressive in all that God wants me to be,
my ugliness and unpleasant nature is never so great, but that God screams for me a different fate.

With God I am:

Reverent, filled with respect and love for a God whom I fear, yet know through obedience, He will draw near.

Right Choices:

Think about Him today with a mixed feeling of reverence, fear, and wonder, caused by something divine (see Deuteronomy 28:58).

MARCH 4 – GOD IS PURE

The Bible says, "Blessed are the pure in heart, for they will see God" (Matthew 5:8).

Pure, how can we describe something we can't begin to comprehend with our finite minds, except to say - He is Holy!

Without God I am:

Polluted, with a bunch of "stuff" that on a hazy day may make sense to the casual observer, when I'm not in want - all is well

With God I am:

Purified, the bad stuff has been filtered out by the Love of Jesus, gone as far as the east is from the west, now if only I can forgive myself - God expects and demands it

Right Choices:

To what can I liken this, pure, like the smile of a newborn baby – the fragrance of a flower in full bloom, the splendor of the vast Rocky Mountains, all fall short, but you get the idea. Be a little "pure" today for someone close to you (see Psalm 19:8).

March 5 – God is Goodness

The Bible says, "I am the good shepherd. The good shepherd lays down his life for the sheep" (John 10:11).

Goodness, why would God die for me, what is it that He sees in me that I don't? This amazing God has made a plan to use you and me to further His Kingdom.

Without God I am:

Good, for what enables me, no plan but my own to carry on, let's sing this song and be gone.

With God I am:

Good, at what I think than more often do, I humbly confess my meager ways, praising God for the good and bad in my days -for it's when I'm groaning - I'm growing.

Right Choices:

I'm struck by why bad things happen to good people. I ask myself the "whys" of my life and wonder. You may do the same. Here is the answer: We are not the author of our lives – God is. He's God, we are not. He makes all things work together for good. That's it....nothing more, but it doesn't make us feel any better, and it takes time. In eternity we'll get over it. Today I'll think about the "goodness" of God and all He has done (see Romans 8:28).

March 6 – God is Compassionate

The Bible says, "Finally, all of you, live in harmony with one another; be sympathetic, love as brothers, be compassionate and humble" (1 Peter 3:8).

Compassionate, though God exists through eternity, our days' number but a few in this life - full of strife, heirs to a fallen path, destined to face wrath - accept Jesus Christ and life.

Without God I am:

Passionate, about life and all that it offers, my senses get confused and lust for more - money, pride, and power number one, two, and three. Jesus is not for me.

With God I am:

Passionate, about life and all that it offers, my senses see what wants to be, but my Spirit sets me free; Thank you, God for loving me!

Right Choices:

When I'm lazy about something, like losing weight, it just doesn't happen. Let "passion" reign and fuel the fires of "desire,", now I'm talking about something man – stand back. Something is going to happen, get fired up (see James 5:11)!

March 7 – God is Gracious

The Bible says, "But because of his great love for us, God, who is rich in mercy, made us alive with Christ even when we were dead in transgressions--it is by grace you have been saved" (Ephesians 2:4-5).

Gracious, how much has God-given and why for me, my stench, awfulness and lowliness scream don't come to me, yet He comes ready to forgive and forget, Jesus Christ has paid the debt

Without God I am:

Gracious, in my own ways toward loving others and caring for needs, God would only ask that I remove the mask, and let Him love me

With God I am:

Gracious, a new found love in Him indeed, caring for and loving others is my daily need, Thank you, Jesus for using me, helping others to see

Right Choices:

Give something special to another today. Now, think about how God gives to you, what have you done lately to let Him know how much you appreciate it? Give thanks (see Psalm 86:15).

March 8 – God is Patient

The Bible says, "And the Lord's servant must not quarrel; instead, he must be kind to everyone, able to teach, not resentful" (2 Timothy 2:2).

Patient, waiting anxiously that none would be lost; a sense of urgency is growing, for believers are-knowing. His return is imminent.

Without God I am:

Impatient, it's difficult when I'm not in control, my life is run on flipping switches to light, pushing buttons to turn on -
getting instant results, don't delay my life - I have no faults.

With God I am:

Patient, my needs and trials seem ever long, I want them to be gone, but God says you have much to learn, let your Spirit grow and earn -
Holiness, Goodness, and Kindness.

Right Choices:

I'm thinking of the poster I saw in the 60's of a vulture sitting up high on a rocky cliff, with the subtitle, "patience my rear end, I'm going to kill something. J Slow down, take it in time – it's the cautious way, safer for sure (see Psalm 40:1).

March 9 – God is Generous

The Bible says. "You will be made rich in every way so that you can be generous on every occasion, and through us your generosity will result in thanksgiving to God" (2 Corinthians 9:11).

Generous, the abundant life is different for God, He is more interested in who we are than in what we have.

Without God I am:

Generous, sparingly, I give what I can afford to lose, to people and places that I choose.

With God I am:

Generous, all that I am and all that I have belong to God, may I desire be to look beyond me, measure my life by the things I gave away - mostly just me.

Right Choices:

An elderly friend of mine when I was a kid growing up said one day as he was fixing a flat tire in his service station. "The only things you take with you out of this life when you leave, are the things you gave away." I'll never forget that day and what he said (see Proverbs 37:26).

March 10 – God is Precious

The Bible says, "Through these he has given us his very great and precious promises, so that through them you may participate in the divine nature and escape the corruption in the world caused by evil desires" (2 Peter 1:4).

Precious, for what would we have if God never was, nothing but emptiness and darkness through all eternity, but in a moment of time, He made us, in His likeness and a little lower than the angels.

Without God I am:

Precious, in His sight and He longs to hold this heart in His hand to mold, more valuable than gold, come quickly to His fold.

With God I am:

Precious, to God and His divine plan, this little life seems so small, I reach out to my fellow man, enabled by God to be all I can be.

Right Choices:

God doesn't make junk, so why do I feel so cheap sometimes? Thinking errors, that's all it is, think right (see Proverb 1:13)!

March 11 – God is Abiding

The Bible says, "For you did not receive a spirit that makes you a slave again to fear, but you received the Spirit of son-ship. And by him we cry, "Abba, Father"'" (Romans 8:15).

Abiding, in the lives of all believers through His Holy Spirit, given as a gift and inheritance to be, life eternal in Glory with God forever free.

Without God I am:

Abiding, in the hope that seems so unsure, my life and tensions begin to blur, what is it that makes the Christian so calm, I feel my life is a time bomb.

With God I am:

Abiding, in the knowledge and grace of Jesus Christ, my assurance divine and mine, to have and to hold from this day forward – sublime.

Right Choices:

So what ideas are you "abiding" in today that may carry you to places you don't want to go; abide in the "vine" and stay "divine." (see - John 15:4).

March 12 – God is Tender

The Bible says, "If you have any encouragement from being united with Christ, if any comfort from his love, if any fellowship with the Spirit, if any tenderness and compassion, then make my joy complete by being like-minded, having the same love, being one in spirit and purpose" (Philippians 2:1-2).

Tender, yet mighty and strong His greatness so immense that He bends His knee to hear, the quiet voice of a child who is very dear and near.

Without God I am:

Tender, in love to those close to me, I respect what I know will be, caring and compassionate people tending to me.

With God I am:

Tender, sensitive, and caring to those in need, I listen carefully to His desire for me to knead, the mixture of life's toils, loves, and blessings into a spiritual feed.

Right Choices:

Here is a challenge for you today, just for the "heck of it," bring someone you care about some flowers with a note telling them how much you care about them – yeah baby (see Psalm 119:156)!

MARCH 13 – GOD IS JOY

The Bible says, "But the fruit of the Spirit is love, joy, peace, patience, kindness, goodness, faithfulness, gentleness and self-control. Against such things there is no law" (Galatians 5:22-23).

Joy, like low hanging fruit, God fills this life with all goodness to be picked, enjoyed, and given away.

Without God I am:

Joyless, a word not often fixed upon, seems religious-oriented and long gone, not often seen on faces near, most people I know are full of fear.

With God I am:

Joyful, when in my heart, I genuinely confess, this God is quick to bless, and guide my heart to glory be, setting my heart totally free to love God - draw near to me.

Right Choices:

Joy is difficult for most of us, it just seems weird to be joyful, know what I mean? I need to worry and be anxious, it really makes things happen...sure it does? So, why don't we ask the Lord for a little joy today – why not (see Mathew 25:21)?

MARCH 14 – GOD IS WORSHIPPED

The Bible says, "Yet a time is coming and has now come when the true worshipers will worship the Father in spirit and truth, for they are the kind of worshipers the Father seeks" (John 4:23).

Worshipped, and to be praised throughout eternity, He is that we are, forever we honor and obey the very God that made us be, sacrificially giving to Him.

Without God I am:

Worshipped, by myself in a sense that I am my own god,
that no other reigns above me, I'm responsible to no higher
standard or calling, society sets my norm.

With God I am:

Worshipful, of a God who I know, is real in my life and the lives of others, this all has not happened by mere chance, praise God for He first loved me, oh that I would see Him more clearly.

Right Choices:

Why does God seek worshipers who seek Him in the spirit? When we are one with the spirit, we are one with the Lord, that's as close to truth as one can get, be close (see 1 Corinthians 14:26).

March 15 – God is Adorned

The Bible says, "Your statutes stand firm; holiness adorns your house for endless days, O LORD" (Psalm 93:5).

Adorned, all creation cries out the adornment of God, His splendor is radiant in the sunset and sunrise alike, beginning and ending - oh what a Friend.

Without God I am:

Adorned, by those I encourage to empower me, my outward appearance is to be envied and cries, "don't you wish you were me" if only we could see - the real "me."

With God I am:

Adoring, His Kingship over my life, the majesty of who He is to me, and the way He has changed my life.

Right Choices:

This looks like appreciate, have reverence, be thankful, value, treasured, something very special – trust that the Lord is all this for you today (see 1 Peter 3:4).

March 16 – God is Sinless

The Bible says, "But you know that he appeared so that he might take away our sins. And in him is no sin" (1 John 3:5).

Sinless, He was tempted in the desert and the mountain top,
He claimed His desires were not the things of this world
but to do the will of His Father, who sent Him.

Without God I am:

Sinful, all that I see is all that I know, I know not that I seek not, so how can this be wrong, just listen to God's whispers
and His Heavenly song.

With God I am:

Sinful, wanting to do what is right, I try with all my might,
but I do wrong because I'm not strong, God says yield to me, and I will set you free.

Right Choices:

It seems distant most times, most Christians don't want to be – it sounds crazy, but it's true. We treasure the morsels of self-indulgence, but only because our nature is sinful – the spiritual man has risen above, remember who you are. God says anything is possible with Me (see - Psalm 28:7)!

March 17 – God is Truth

The Bible says, "God did this so that, by two unchangeable things in which it is impossible for God to lie, we who have fled to take hold of the hope offered to us may be greatly encouraged" (Hebrews 6:18).

Truth, His words revealed in the Bible are inerrant, all that He is infallible – "how do we know?" asks the fool of the wise man. The wise replied, "this is true because the mystery of His wonder says so."

Without God I am:

Living a Lie, deceived by temporary powers, the flowers of the hour seems right for me, their fragrance so fine, my life is mine, I'm doing just fine.

With God I am:

Truthful, gone are the sins of past, my secret life revealed, at last, forgiven and yearning to be whole, my innocence that Satan stole, restored anew by His Holly hand, now take a stand and hold this hand.

Right Choices:

What is truth the sinner says? What would you say to the question of death, will you one day die? So, what's next (see 2 Timothy 2:15)?

March 18 – God is Unashamed

The Bible says, "And now, dear children, continue in him, so that when he appears we may be confident and unashamed before him at his coming" (1John 2:28).

Unashamed, He has done no wrong to anyone, He wants only what is right for any of us, His existence is perfect forever past, present and ever to be - He has done no wrong.

Without God I am:

Shameful, all that I am is inherently evil, fallen to a lower nature from God's Holy plan, may I take His hand and leave this unholy land, take a second look at His Holy Book - The Bible.

With God I am:

Shameless, washed white as snow by God's forgiveness, now I must forget as God has forgotten, casting my remembrances to God, not letting Satan take away my repentance.

Right Choices:

Being unashamed frees one from condemnation; it's a good thing. Be shameless today in all you think, do and say (see Romans 8:1).

March 19 – God is Assurance

The Bible says, "Those who have served well gain an excellent standing and great assurance in their faith in Christ Jesus" (1 Timothy 3:13).

Assurance, He has made a plan that is right and good for all, but we choose another way, causing us to pay.

Without God I am:

Assured, by things of this world - my portfolio, my assets, my health, my loves, my good looks, my fun, my wisdom, yes - life is good to me.

With God I am:

Assured, I know in my heart that what is happening to me is for my ultimate good, God asks that I pause here to learn a bit more, letting my faith rescue me and adore a God who is good.

Right Choices:

You can hold your head high today, confident that this God is on your side. Doing more than you can imagine to help you (see 1 Timothy 3:13)!

MARCH 20 – GOD IS TRANSFORMING

The Bible says, "Do not conform any longer to the pattern of this world, but be transformed by the renewing of your mind. Then you will be able to test and approve what God's will is--his good, pleasing and perfect will" (Romans 12:2).

Transforming, as we surrender to His presence, His power affects our soul and our senses know His very essence.

Without God I am:

Transitioned, from phase to phase of my life so that as I think and grow I become, numb to the things of God - I succumb.

With God I am:

Transformed, by the effect of God's power, my mind - heart - and soul are changed, He takes my will, enables me to love, never the same, loss of shame.

Right Choices:

Just remember, God is changing you and transforming you into His person, it's not in your striving, but in your surrender. Be surrendered today – big time (see Hebrews 10:14)!

March 21 – God is Enduring

The Bible says, "May the God who gives endurance and encouragement give you a spirit of unity among yourselves as you follow Christ Jesus, so that with one heart and mouth you may glorify the God and Father of our
Lord Jesus Christ" (Romans 15:5,6).

Enduring, God is that He is, He desires every person created to live with Him in eternity, He stands at the door of our hearts and knocks, saying "Let Me enter in."

Without God I am:

Endurable, this battle is mine, I'll stand to the end, fraught with despair, my heart will never mend.

With God I am:

Enduring, the race seems long, and I'm weary in a pit, life calls for me to quit - end it all now, pain, distress, fatigue, and hardship seem all that I have, enter Lord Jesus, and be my salve.

Right Choices:

While what I'm going through now seems like eternity, I want it to end, and it will. God will help you endure, because that is who He is, an Enduring God (see - Proverbs 8:18)!

MARCH 22 – GOD IS UNSELFISH

The Bible says, "Do nothing out of selfish ambition or vain conceit, but in humility consider others better than yourselves" (Philippians 2:3).

Unselfish, He owns it all and gives it all to all as He sees need. We plead to God - give me, give me ---- He wants to give us Himself - more than things.

Without God I am:

Selfish, wanting more of what I have and don't have,
enough never seems adequate, I horde my "stuff" to seal my fate.

With God I am:

Giving, my time, talent, money, and most importantly my love, that comes from above like a descending dove.

Right Choices:

This is just about impossible. In any one day, I have 950,400 seconds. I figure about 950,000 of those I'm thinking about me. Be generous today, give someone 1,000 seconds today (see James 3:16).

March 23 – God is Our Guide

The Bible says, "He guides the humble in what is right and teaches them his way" (Psalm 25:9).

Guide, We plan our ways but He directs our steps, His
light on our path guiding us Home, He will never leave us alone.

Without God I am:

Guided, by things of importance and daily matters, my life
feels I have too much on my platter, I seek for priorities to rule my
life, but it brings me each day more and more strife.

With God I am:

Guided, assured by my daily prayers that this is right,
I put on my full armor to begin my daily fight.

Right Choices:

The neat thing about a guide is you just let them lead and you follow
along. So, what's so hard about that? Be a willing follower today.
He'll take you to good places (see Psalm 23:3)!

March 24 – God is Revealed

The Bible says, "I have revealed and saved and proclaimed I, and not some foreign god among you. You are my witnesses," declares the LORD, "that I am God" (Isaiah 43:12).

Revealed, through His Son Jesus Christ, through the splendor of His creation and through the amazement
of my intricate self.

Without God I am:

Revealed, for who and what I have become, like debris floating to the surface of my life, are the things and effects of what I have done.

With God I am:

Revealed, for who and what I am in Christ, my life not perfect but forgiven by Him, I thirst for Him abiding within.

Right Choices:

Some like to keep their life private, even secret. Tell a good friend a secret sin of yours today, and see what the Lord does with that (see Romans 1:17).

March 25 – God is Sustainer

The Bible says, "Even to your old age and gray hairs I am he, I am he who will sustain you. I have made you and I will carry you; I will sustain you and I will rescue you" (Isaiah 46:4).

Sustainer, yes - He sustains those who love Him, but what He really wants to do is grow us, out of the mundane and into an incredible being, seeing, and believing.

Without God I am:

Sustained, by the confidence in me, my work, my bank account, portfolio, my daily living and attainment.

With God I am:

Sustained, by the assurance of a Living God who is redeeming a piece of my mind, heart, and soul each day, winning back ground lost to my selfish ways.

Right Choices:

When the gas in the tank seems about gone, and you're looking for some fuel – shoot up a quick prayer today, and you will be amazed by what happens (see Psalms 55:22)!

MARCH 26 – GOD IS PAVILION

The Bible says, "Who can understand how he spreads out the clouds, how he thunders from his pavilion" (Job 36:29)?

Pavilion, His Holy framework is a majestic structure around all the believers. When God looks, He sees a mighty fortress protecting His loved ones both near and far.

Without God I am:

Protected, for now by what seems secure, I lock my doors, nail down my hatches, I don't talk to strangers and avoid all dangers, never to get off track or be lured.

With God I am:

Protected, by Angels who stand guard, His arms always go below where I am to catch me, never so low to go, that God's Love can't take me in tow.

Right Choices:

If we could see the vast array of spiritual forces protecting our everyday lives, we would stand in awe. Don't feel alone today, God is with you (see Psalm 27:5)!

March 27– God is Our Refuge

The Bible says, "Have mercy on me, O God, have mercy on me, for in you my soul takes refuge. I will take refuge in the shadow of your wings until the disaster has passed (Psalm 57:1).

Refuge, this Holy place is calm amid the storm, a safe place of comfort - our mind is at ease and a great God is pleased. We are welcome here in this Holy court.

Without God I am:

Hiding, in a place where I feel safe, I cling with white knuckles in fear, to "things" that might be taken that are dear, oh that this would pass my place clear.

With God I am:

Hiding, in the shadows of God Almighty, His shadow cast a fate across my life, protecting me from strife.

Right Choices:

The shadow of God is immense and all powerful because it is holy, mighty, and all loving to the marrow of my bone. You will know you are standing in it when the heat comes (see Psalm 59:16).

March 28 – God is Adorable

The Bible says, "O LORD, God of our fathers, are you not the God who is in heaven? You rule over all the kingdoms of the nations. Power and might are in your hand, and no one can withstand you" (2 Chronicles 20:6).

Adorable, seems such a trite word, but it is true, all that is lovely, all that is true, is certainly to be beheld and to be loved too.

Without God I am:

Adorned, with beauty and riches that seem so fresh, I have been truly blessed by what great provider and for what purpose I ask, just let me conqueror another task.

With God I am:

Adorned, with the peace that passes all understanding,
a humble heart and a desire to know the Lord, He takes away all my discord.

Right Choices:

To be adorable is to adorn the graciousness of God; it is what God wants each of us to do, daily (see Psalm 93:5).

MARCH 29 – GOD IS LOVELINESS

The Bible says, "This is love: not that we loved God, but that he loved us and sent his Son as an atoning sacrifice for our sins" (1 John 4:10).

Loveliness, in reverent awe, we gaze upon a God who is the essence of love. Bowed low we go, with Him who fights our foe.

Without God I am:

Loved, by myself to such a great extent, collecting many things everywhere I went, I long to be satisfied when I am only gratified.

With God I am:

Loving, to those in need and others who have wants, I give a caring ear and draw near, listening to His whispering voice, He gives me another choice.

Right Choices:

To be lovely is to love, be the mirror of God's love today (see Colossians 1:4).

March 30 – God is Contentment

The Bible says, "Keep your lives free from the love of money and be content with what you have, because God has said, "Never will I leave you; never will I forsake you" (Hebrews 13:5).

Contentment, only one thing that God desires more, and that is for my heart to yearn for and love Him more.

Without God I am:

Content, with the fact that my life lacks meaning, I push to the point of screaming, my life is a mess, I must confess.

With God I am:

Content, more often in my mind then in my heart, I look for the "quick hit" to lift me higher, did it really help - you liar.

Right Choices:

Someone once said, "contentment is wanting what we have." It's ok to want things, seek them with the "spirits" guiding hand (see 1Timothy 6:6).

March 31 – God is Satisfying

The Bible says, "And I--in righteousness I will see your face; when I awake, I will be satisfied with seeing your likeness" (Psalm 17:15).

Satisfying, what is it about this Holy God that soothes the soul and calms the spirit, all for need, want or desire, we would aspire - Him.

Without God I am:

Satisfied, I feel good today my stomach is full, my passions are dull, sun on my face feeling no disgrace, let's get up and go run this race - to another place.

With God I am:

Satisfied, all that I am and all that I have are found in Him. He gives abundantly that we would win a heart that is true, caring, and loving to all of you.

Right Choices:

Oh how we long to be satisfied, the cravings that have no end. At the very top of the pile is to be god, god of my life, at the bottom to serve a holy God as a slave. Turn the pyramid upside down today, and look at this anew (see Proverbs 13:25)!

April 1 – God is Reflected

The Bible says, "As water reflects a face, so a man's heart reflects the man" (Proverbs 27:19).

Reflected, in the majesty and beauty of His creation, His laws written on our hearts so that none could say, You were away, I knew you not, take not my name from the "Book of Life" - a blot.

Without God I am:

Reflected, I look in the mirror and what do I see, a person who I barely recognize - is this really me, how did my life go this way, now in eternity I must pay.

With God I am:

Reflected, in the eyes which mirror the soul, His plan is all part of my life's goals, to grow in Him each day, and make Him known by how I play and what I say.

Right Choices:

Be a reflection today of all that God has made you by simply saying ; "Thank you" Jesus (see Colossians 3:16).

April 2 – God is Splendid

The Bible says, "He said: "O LORD, God of Israel, there is no God like you in heaven or on earth--you who keep your covenant of love with your servants who continue wholeheartedly in your way" (2 Chronicles 6:14).

Splendid, to the addict, our desire would be to get "drunk" on the wonder of God, to over indulge this amazing experience. Addict our wills Lord, make us splendid in your sight.

Without God I am:

Splendid, most days seem average, but once in a blue moon, but never too soon, I catch a moment of time,
that is truly sublime.

With God I am:

Splendid, as a gift offering from heaven for obedience lived, the fragrance of my life is right, always a delight,
my future is bright.

Right Choices:

Continue wholeheartedly in the way you want to be remembered by your peers, as they reflect around the camp fire of your life about you (see 1 Kings8:23).

April 3 – God is Infinite

The Bible says, "and to know this love that surpasses knowledge--that you may be filled to the measure of all the fullness of God" (Ephesians 3:19).

Infinite, in power, wisdom and ability, He reveals all that He is in small portions to those He uses, unveiling a plan as He chooses.

Without God I am:

Finite, how big can I get, how long will I live, seems
adequate to me, but only if I could see, what could be in eternity.

With God I am:

Finite, glimpses of God through a narrow door, enable my
life to explore, the grandeur of a God, who is sparing me the rod,
destined to embrace His infinite grace.

Right Choices:

How does a finite mind grasp an infinite God? It's easy, one blessing at a time (see Psalm 147:5)!

April 4 – God is Trustworthy

The Bible says, "The law of the LORD is perfect, reviving the soul. The statutes of the LORD are trustworthy, making wise the simple" (Psalm 19:7).

Trustworthy, for God who is the living force, no other power can over tower, He speaks and it is, behold this God portions to those He uses, unveiling a plan as He chooses.

Without God I am:

Trusted, by others who hope obligations are met, I struggle with all my debt, and look for ways to wiggle out, casting fear, gloom and doubt – about.

With God I am:

Trusted, by others who know my word is clear, guided by a God who is very near and dear, I live a good life, causing little strife.

Right Choice:

If you trust the Lord, be as you would expect the Lord to be with you, as you build trust with others (see Revelation 22:6)

April 5 – God is Blessing

The Bible says" "Blessed is the man who does not walk in the counsel of the wicked or stand in the way of sinners or sit in the seat of mockers. But his delight is in the law of the LORD, and on his law he meditates day and night (Psalms 1:1,2).

Blessing, His goodness and rightness He desires all to have,
He bestows it on all He chooses like a welcome salve, all part of the Divine plan, His gracious hand offered to man.

Without God I am:

Blessed, by things that God has given, knowledge, power and wisdom all from Him and driven, that one day I might see, the glory of a God given for me - come onto Thee.

With God I am:

Blessed, by the very nature of God who is great, I feel His presence like the warm sun, soothing my soul for a day of fun, my destiny today to love and not wait.

Right Choices:

As a blessing is a divine favor, seek today to favor a loved one with no strings attached (see Ephesians 1:3)

APRIL 6 – GOD IS HUMBLE

The Bible says, "Then Christ would have had to suffer many times since the creation of the world. But now he has appeared once for all at the end of the ages to do away with sin by the sacrifice of himself" (Hebrews 9:26).

Humble, how can and why should a God who is so amazing be humble, what is He humbled by and to whom, the answer is simply this, He hung on a tree for you and me.

Without God I am:

Humbled, by the knowledge of my own limitations and what I see in others be, the challenge is great but I charge out the gate, failure seals my fate.

With God I am:

Humbled, empowered from above, I yearn for His love, my importance to God is not based on what I have done, but what I've become.

Right Choices:

Why does pride feel so good, and why does God hate it so much? At the root of it all it screams for independence from God - that's a problem (see 1 Peter 5:5)!

April 7 – God is Demanding

The Bible says, "Jesus replied: "Love the Lord your God with all your heart and with all your soul and with all your mind. This is the first and greatest commandment" (Mathew 22:37,38).

Demanding, "Do not let the word of God depart from your lips" (Isaiah 59:21) let your yes be yes and your no be no, repent and sin no more - He said it and He expects it.

Without God I am:

Demanded, to be so many things to so many people, to whom do I say "yes" today? This life is crazy all the way.

With God I am:

Demanded, to be directionally correct, Heaven bound – standing on solid ground, how I think - what I say and do,
let my mind each day be renewed - Jesus loves me too.

Right Choices:

Would a general win a war if he were not demanding? No, of course not! God's at war for your heart, the consequences are immense, for you (see Genesis 9:5)!

April 8 – God is Radiant

The Bible says, "The precepts of the LORD are right, giving joy to the heart. The commands of the LORD are radiant, giving light to the eyes" (Psalms 19:8).

Radiant, what is it that makes the goodness of God shine, like the morning dew on a silver leaf, the sparkle in ocean foam at night, our love shines through to His delight.

Without God I am:

Radiating, the essence of who I am, sometimes I simply just don't give a hoot, I run from fire to fire, ready to fall from this tight wire.

With God I am:

Radiating, from battle; the will to do right that starts in the mind, this God empowers every time, we seek a righteous path, I did the math - what did it cost, my own life lost at last.

Right Choices:

Be radiant with hope today, for the victory over the temptation that is driving you crazy (see Psalm 19:8).

April 9 – God is Enabled

The Bible says, "Whoever believes in the Son has eternal life, but whoever rejects the Son will not see life, for God's wrath remains on him" (John 3:36).

Enabled, by a Holiness and Eternal goodness that has no beginning or end, this God came here to send, all to a Heavenly place, so get ready to run the race.

Without God I am:

Enabling, my life to tell a story giving myself all the glory, look and see what I have done, my only regret in the end, I never knew the Son.

With God I am:

Enabling, my life to be a witness for Him, I take to the Cross all my sin, daily keeping my talk and walk in pace, to win the race.

Right Choices:

This is one of the most profound truths in all scripture that God enables. You need to spend 15 minutes today thinking about how God has enabled you. After that, spend the rest of your life "Thanking" Him (see Leviticus 26:13)!

APRIL 10 – GOD IS UNDERSTANDING

The Bible says, "The LORD looks down from heaven on the sons of men to see if there are any who understand, any who seek God" (Psalms 14:2).

Understanding, He walked this earth and was tempted but was sinless in all ways, He watches all through every day, knowing the trials we have within, desiring that none would sin.

Without God I am:

Understanding, and knowing at times I should be more bestowing, it only matters that things keep flowing, more to get done, I'm on the run.

With God I am:

Understanding, I wish more at times to know, that when God says I am Peace, that I feel Peaceful, I am Joy, that I feel Joyful, I am Forgiven, that I feel washed clean - Amen.

Right Choices:

You want to keep a secret from God, ha….might as well want to fly as well. God knit you together in your mother's womb. Every crevice and cell of your being, he knows. It's ok, God will meet you where you are, right now (see Matthew 6:8).

April 11 – God is Cleansing

The Bible says, "let us draw near to God with a sincere heart in full assurance of faith, having our hearts sprinkled to cleanse us from a guilty conscience and having our bodies washed with pure water" (Hebrew 10:22)

Cleansing, His forgiveness is quick and sure, gone with a blur, sin never to be remembered, repent now and let Me help you win the war.

Without God I am:

Soiled, with the spots and affects of sin, my soul heavy burdened within, I see inside who I am now, Jesus is ready for me to bow, come behold - take hold this Son, stop the running and come.

With God I am:

Cleaned, white as snow by His cleansing blood, Jesus the ultimate sacrifice for past - present - and future sins, daily I come to Him, confessing - repentant in heart, each day a new start.

Right Choices:

"Twenty Mule Team Borax" could not clean up a mess as quickly as God can answer a simple prayer of confession (see Ephesians 5:26).

April 12 – God is Eternal

The Bible says, "Lord, you have been our dwelling place throughout all generations. 2Before the mountains were born or you brought forth the earth and the world, from everlasting to everlasting you are God" (Psalms 90:1,2).

Eternal, how long is forever, can the mind begin to grasp,
unchanging and timeless He always will be, hard to
imagine how God can be, oh how our heart's long to see.

Without God I am:

In-Eternity, forever destined at days end last, died into slavery for sins of past, agonizing in total fear, wishing those Christians had come nearer, to share Faith and Love, from Jesus above.

With God I am:

In-Eternity, forever destined at days end last, died into glory with all sins forgiven past, rejoicing in total cheer, so Thankful for those who were near, to share Faith and Love from Jesus above.

Right Choices:

Like the last spoonful of your very best dessert, imagine something so good never ending; rejoice today in the Lord (see Psalm 111:110).

APRIL 13 – GOD IS SAVIOR

The Bible says, "For God so loved the world that he gave his one and only Son, that whoever believes in him shall not perish but have eternal life" (John 3:16).

Savior, saved "from what" the fool may ask us, I simply don't understand all the fuss, yes - truly this is the case, but God knew better and sent His Son, that none would be lost but won.

Without God I am:

Lost, to an evilness that lurks behind scenes, poking and pulling my will until it screams, at the horror my heart melts down, it's too late now to turn around.

With God I am:

Saved, by a willingness to choose each day, the love of a Savior who had a better way, given to be a sinful man, Jesus came to offer His hand, enabling me to take a stand.

Right Choices:

You know the best part of this for us now is this, we are being spared the consequences of a life gone wrong – heaven on earth, as good as it gets on this side (see Psalm 25:5).

April 14 – God is Affirmation

The Bible says, "God said to Moses, "I AM WHO I AM. This is what you are to say to the Israelites: "I AM has sent me to you" (Exodus 3:14).

Affirmation, that He is who He is, and does what He does,
our response to be, to take and see clear, that which is given - take and behold is striven, to make us better to the letter.

Without God I am:

Affirming, that which is and seems to be in my life, the
good and bad with all the strife, to carry me forward on the plan,
I'll remain dogged and take my stand.

With God I am:

Affirming, that I am fallible and weak, to this dear Lord I seek, to make me strong, leading me on, daily pausing to adorn, this wonderful God who makes me reborn.

Right Choices:

This is the deal, yes, we are free to have our way, our own thoughts, but at the end of the day, it only leads to hell (see 1 John 5:13).

APRIL 15 – GOD IS COMING

The Bible says, "while we wait for the blessed hope--the glorious appearing of our great God and Savior, Jesus Christ, who gave himself for us to redeem us from all wickedness and to purify for himself a people that are his very own, eager to do what is good" (Titus 2:13,14).

Coming, what is a day on God's clock, one little tick-tock,
the sound is deafening but I hear Him not, all Glory shall shone,
as He comes to take us home, be ready the hour is near, don't fear.

Without God I am:

Going, to places with gnashing of teeth, pleading my case beneath, tons of evidence of sin, all held within.

With God I am:

Going, to a place where I get a new body, recognizable but pure, gold paved streets and a place prepared for me not shoddy, worshipping God all the day long, in word and song.

Right Choices:

Coming ever so close daily to reveal His spirit and bless this life, draw close today with special thankfulness (see Ezekiel 43:2).

APRIL 16 – GOD IS EXALTED

The Bible says, "Therefore God exalted him to the highest place and gave him the name that is above every name, that at the name of Jesus every knee should bow, in heaven and on earth and under the earth, and every tongue confess that Jesus Christ is Lord, to the glory of God the Father" (Philippians 2:9-11).

Exalted, by the beauty of His creation, by the scent of a rose, the sun as it rose, a brand new day for us to pray,
this amazing God is on display.

Without God I am:

Exalting, the essence of who I am and what I've done,
I can't believe I'm having so much fun, I just don't have time for the Son.

With God I am:

Exalting, this amazing God who cares so much for me,
He guides my hand and helps me to see, I praise Him for keeping me from sin, this relationship is win - win.

Right Choices:

Exalting us to new understanding and belief; enabling this feeble soul as we look to the "source" for "strength" (see Job 36:22).

April 17 – God is Spirit

The Bible says, "Don't you know that you yourselves are God's temple and that God's Spirit lives in you (1Corinthians 3:16)?

Spirit, God is closer than the air we breathe, His Holy Spirit in union with our soul, talking as one to guide the heart and mind toward a place which is Heavenly Divine.

Without God I am:

Spirit, caught in a web where evil comes, the spider spirit lingers until the battle is won, to devour his prey and cast me away, eternally tormented in Hell.

With God I am:

Spirit, He comes to me, a mystery and union I cannot
see, but it's real - I feel, Him guiding, assuring and enabling me within, He steers me away from the web of sin.

Right Choices:

We can't begin to grasp the essence and content of this "spirit" until we begin to see it move our thinking from a former place to a better place, almost without reason (see Romans 14:17).

April 18 – God is Fair Minded

The Bible says, "Masters, provide your slaves with what is right and fair, because you know that you also have a Master in heaven" (Colossians 4:1).

Fair minded, His measure has no bias, His judgment is ultimately pure and not pious, for all alike we are of one skin, to Him sin is sin, He calls all men to Him - (mankind).

Without God I am:

Fair, in how the rules are made but not played, I'll stretch my actions to favor me and cry "foul" hoping to get paid, winning a point in the game, all I want to do is defame.

With God I am:

Fair, wanting for others how I would want for me, desiring no advantage for He, has a plan that will benefit those who believe, my life of good and bad a blanket of warmth He weaves.

Right Choices:

Impartially God leads in one accord, remember, the most important thing about me is what I think about God. His justice and righteousness endures, be likewise to others today (see Acts 17:11).

April 19 – God is Giving

The Bible says, "Remember this: Whoever sows sparingly will also reap sparingly, and whoever sows generously will also reap generously" (2 Corinthians 9:6).

Giving, such a glorious life for all to share, His creation, family, friends and moments to use the senses, to dwell on His richness and to enjoy and be thankful.

Without God I am:

Thankful, for the pay off my hard work has obtained, I continue to seek gain, I know not where all this good luck comes, chance to say, it all just happens that way.

With God I am:

Thankful, specifically to a God who I know cares and has given to me such an abundance of blessing, I know the Source and the Source knows me and I am thankful to Him.

Right Choices:

Something about "giving" that purifies the flowing out and flowing in, one blessing another. Don't stagnate today, flow your goodness everywhere (see Psalm 95:2).

APRIL 20 – GOD IS DESERVING

The Bible says, "15and if you reject my decrees and abhor my laws and fail to carry out all my commands and so violate my covenant, 16then I will do this to you: I will bring upon you sudden terror, wasting diseases and fever that will destroy your sight and drain away your life. You will plant seed in vain, because your enemies will eat it" (Leviticus 26:15-16).

Deserving, that we humbly confess but we fail to draw near, we just don't seem to care or understand how dear, this Lord is that created me, and died to set me free.

Without God I am:

Deserving, Hell for my lack of belief, faith, obedience and trusting God, He loves this soul and spares the rod, if His patience could be heard, the roar would be terror stirred.

With God I am:

Deserving, Hell for my shallow belief, disobedience and sinfulness, lacking to confess, Oh but grace has come today, Praise God who helps me pray.

Right Choices:

Let your heart deserve God today (see Luke 12:48).

April 21 – God is Reason

The Bible says, "The thief comes only to steal and kill and destroy; I have come that they may have life, and have it to the full" (John 10:10).

Reason, for the Season, He has come to give us all a better life, not only in the after-life, but now throughout each day, we pray that He keep the enemy at bay.

Without God I am:

Reasoned, to be readily sure, that all my plans are in my hands, some days I wonder what it's all about, maybe I'll just sit and pout.

With God I am:

Reasoned, to the majesty of this great mystery, my life stands in awe of all the history, God has blessed me so much, it's all so amazing from His Blessed Touch.

Right Choices:

Like the "source" that seems to fill a void, but it's more, because it has substance and real experience and meaning – how do I put my finger on it? Why do I need to? Just Believe! Have Faith! Trust! .... obey..... J (see John 10:17).

April 22 – God is Reigning

The Bible says, "The Lord reigns forever, your God, O Zion, for all generations, Praise the Lord (Psalm 146:10).

Reigning, to quiet the souls of the weary, to bring rest and assurance of His love to a life which has become dreary.

Without God I am:

Reigning, in the heyday of my career, no stopping me now for any fear, I'm picking them up and laying them down, man am I going to town.

With God I am:

Reigning, with a Holy God who shares with my spirit, compassion for people who need it, this life a gift to me, to help others that they might see.

Right Choices:

Reigning for sure and that is a good thing – read the newspaper lately? We shake our head and wonder why, on the worst day of my life, if I'm standing in the shadow of God Almighty, I'm in a good place (see Exodus 15:18).

April 23 – God is Accomplished

The Bible says, "LORD, you establish peace for us; all that we have accomplished you have done for us" (Isaiah 26:12).

Accomplished, so much that on the seventh day He rested,
I wonder what He did - from where does God get renewed?
It must be that innate internal Goodness - He rested within.

Without God I am:

Accomplishing, on the outside what is most needed on the inside, that this soul would see Jesus Christ and have a new life.

With God I am:

Accomplishing, victory one thought at a time, when I think anxiety - I think peaceful assurance, when I think lust - I condemn my thought as rape, when I think praise - I see Jesus smiling at me.

Right Choices:

May the Lord be accomplished in my life today (see Deuteronomy 30:1-4).

April 24 – God is Caring

The Bible says, "Cast all your anxiety on him because he cares for you" (1 Peter 5:7).

Caring, why would this God keep track of the number of hairs on my head? He does so because no detail of my life is left un-led.

Without God I am:

Complacent, about those things that don't feed my success, I have my priorities and only so much time, I build resources that shall be mine.

With God I am:

Complacent, I all too often begin to take this awesome God for granted, thinking and doing things abandoned to God, why is it I settle for this shallow pleasing time?

Right Choices:

Anxiety is what we have when we attempt to control an outcome that is beyond our capacity, the point is, He has capacity - give it up (see Deuteronomy 11:12-15).

April 25 – God is a Companion

The Bible says, "A man of many companions may come to ruin, but there is a friend who sticks closer than a brother" (Proverbs 18:24).

A companion, who gave His Son as a Gift from Thee, abiding with these wretched souls - us, going to those who Believe - have Faith - and Trust, as He delivers us from all our lusts.

Without God I am:

In-dwelt, with passions and forces unknown, evil spirits invade my thought life where the battle is won or lost, guided by what they ask? Such a great loss - now who's the boss?

With God I am:

In-dwelt, with passion and forces known, spirits invade my thought life where the battle is won or lost, guided by God and His Love - for He's the boss.

Right Choices:

How close is close when it comes to God as our companion? Give it over to Him and let Him give life (see 1 Corinthians 15:45).

April 26 – God is a King

The Bible says, "By myself I have sworn, my mouth has uttered in all integrity a word that will not be revoked: Before me every knee will bow; by me every tongue will swear. 24They will say of me, 'In the LORD alone are righteousness and strength.' "All who have raged against him will come to him and be put to shame" (Isaiah 45:23-24).

King, seated on a throne, one day every knee will bow and every tongue confess, that Jesus Christ is Lord.

Without God I am:

King, over what I own, my life and those near and dear, I have no fear, this is working for me now, take no other vow.

With God I am:

Kingdom-Bound, not only is this side of eternity better, I read His letter - the Bible - He has me Kingdom-Bound.

Right Choices:

If you wait to crown him king of your life, your life might be over (see 2 Chronicles 1:11).

April 27 – God is A Rock

The Bible says, "The LORD is my rock, my fortress and my deliverer; my God is my rock, in whom I take refuge. He is my shield and the horn of my salvation, my stronghold" (Psalms 18:2).

A rock, this granite be that goes from sea to sea, solid and un-giving, a foundation of believing.

Without God I am:

Standing on shallow ground, it seems firm and not lacking, but the earthquakes of my life cause cracking, will it all fall? I once was standing tall.

With God I am:

Standing on the Rock, firm footed and sure, nothing can lure me away, for God is here to stay.

Right Choices:

Rocks are a solid reminder of the steadfastness of the Lord, it works for him in all ways, who he is, what he does, how he defends and supports – simply solid (see 2 Samuel 22:3).

APRIL 28 – GOD IS GLORY

The Bible says, "Your ways, O God, are holy. What god is so great as our God? 14You are the God who performs miracles; you display your power among the peoples. 15With your mighty arm you redeemed your people, the descendants of Jacob and Joseph" (Psalms 77:13-15).

Glory, who does proclaim for the heavens abound, the story is hidden in an intricate rose and the silent roar of the coming of spring's sound.

Without God I am:

Glorious, this is all so grand, look what I've done across the land, boy I'm good, all that I could - so fine, I shine.

With God I am:

Glorious, the eyes are the mirror of the soul, and this soul is fortified by a Holy Spirit full, of God's love from above.

Right Choices:

Glory doesn't mix with sin and the dark side of anything, so to begin to get close to glory, you had better get right with a Holy God (see -Exodus 15:11).

April 29 – God is The Way

The Bible says, "As for God, his way is perfect; the word of the LORD is flawless. He is a shield for all who take refuge in him" (Psalm 18:30).

The way, what is the importance of something we can do without?
My choice to live without, but oh if I could see,
the battle that rages for me - my soul.

Without God I am:

My way, practical choices that only make sense, I'll come to my defense, God! - who is He? I did my stuff for all to see, condemn me not - for my lot.

With God I am:

His way, my sail is in the air, for God to blow it where, He chooses best, I'll be blest.

Right Choices:

Since you must go a "way", why not go the way of the Lord? We all know who is leading the "other" way, and where it is headed – hell (see Mathew 23:33).

April 30 – God is Present

The Bible says, "For since the creation of the world God's invisible qualities--his eternal power and divine nature--have been clearly seen, being understood from what has been made, so that men are without excuse" (Romans 1:20).

Present, in the universe displayed, the beauty of creation, our amazing body, our heart, mind, soul, Holy Spirit in union with our soul - living within us.

Without God I am:

Abiding, in the realm of my limited understanding, what I know is where I stand, choices influenced by I like who I am.

With God I am:

Abiding, in the quest to know Him better, with each glimpse He gives in His Letter, I feel His presence now, oh wow!

Right Choices:

No one has ever seen God, yet the beauty of God is seen in every day circumstances. Every time today it happens, thank Jesus for letting you glimpse his testimony (see Psalm 89:15).

MAY 1 – GOD IS TIMELESS

The Bible says, "Your word, O LORD, is eternal; it stands firm in the heavens. 90Your faithfulness continues through all generations; you established the earth, and it endures. 91Your laws endure to this day, for all things serve you" (Psalms 119:89-91).

Timeless, for billions of years He planned for today,
that what matters most in this day, the moment and speck of time;
the choices that bind, us to Him in our heart, soul, and mind.

Without God I am:

Timing, my life with the rhythm of each day, sleep - eat - off to work - eat - home - eat - work/relax - sleep - it goes on and the years pass, I wonder how long it will last.

With God I am:

Timing, sometimes I wonder why this is happening to me, what is it that God wants me to see, I want this to pass - fast, but God wants it to last so that I will be - free - at last.

Right Choices:

Don't rush it today, take time to savor the hurt and learn (see Deuteronomy 33:27).

May 2 – God is Wise

The Bible says, "For the wisdom of this world is foolishness in God's sight. As it is written: "He catches the wise in their craftiness"" (1Corinthians 3:19).

Wise, how can we even talk about the wisdom of God, for to Him, our knowledge is so limited, but if we fear and love Him, He will teach us how to be wise within.

Without God I am:

Foolish, because my finite mind is focused on such a limited purpose, if this life were made available to God, He would make it a rose, a lasting beautiful fragrance to behold.

With God I am:

Wise when I cry out daily to a loving God to guide and direct each step of my day to a place where I honor, trust, and obey Him in all that I think, say and do.

Right Choices:

Having trouble today with wrong thoughts, tell a trusted friend and ask them to pray (see Hosea 14:9).

MAY 3 – GOD IS DEPENDABLE

The Bible says, "For no matter how many promises God has made, they are "Yes" in Christ. And so through him the "Amen" is spoken by us to the glory of God" (2 Corinthians 1:20).

Dependable, His yes is yes, and His no is no, Amen means that's the way it's going to be, I said it, that's the end of it. Let's move on.

Without God I am:

Independent, most things are relative to me and I form my own perspective of influence.

With God I am:

Dependent, on a purposeful God who does not tempt me, but tests me by allowing temptation to pull on my will, Jesus gives me the strength to climb this hill.

Right Choices:

God is depending on me today to not let Him down, which means I need to lift Him up and let Him indwell richly – empowering a lowly spirit (see Psalm 25).

MAY 4 – GOD IS PERFECT

The Bible says, "He is the Rock, his works are perfect, and all his ways are just. A faithful God who does no wrong, upright and just is He" (Deuteronomy 32:4).

Perfect, imagine being without blemish, no scars of life – oh, yes, this golden God is real, good as good we can feel,
He's here for us to be healed.

Without God I am:

Imperfect, so I may be, but all others are too, what does it matter to this fool?

With God I am:

Perfected, with the knowledge of Jesus Christ my Savior,
my life has a new flavor: love, hope, peace, joy, belief,
faith, and trust.

Right Choices:

Oh, how I long to be perfect in His sight, how can it be? One might say we are all perfect in His sight, when He sees us as His children – forgiven and free (see Matthew 5:48).

May 5 – God is Appointing

The Bible says, "For we are God's workmanship, created in Christ Jesus to do good works, which God prepared in advance for us to do" (Ephesians 2:10).

Appointing, those as He sees fit, to sit - and take a place,
to be part of His great race - a plan so great, sometimes we have to wait.

Without God I am:

Disappointed, angry and impetuous lies flow, who now has
my soul, what shall I do? - whom can I fool?

With God I am:

Disappointed, why it didn't happen, I expected it to be so,
but who is looking after my soul, it is He, and He only gives what's best for me.

Right Choices:

Appointing means to be given a special position by someone. The Lord is giving as best He sees fit, which may not always lead to me being pleased (see 1 Timothy 1:12).

MAY 6 – GOD IS RESCUER

The Bible says, "Even to your old age and gray hairs I am he, I am he who will sustain you. I have made you and I will carry you; I will sustain you and I will rescue you" (Isaiah 46:4).

Rescuer, He hears and responds to our every call for help,
while it never seems soon enough, He only asks that we trust.

Without God I am:

Abandoned, to a life full of lies and cheating, hate flows and my body is bleeding, losing precious life from all my strife.

With God I am:

Rescued, from the toils of my sin, held within but given to Him, set my mind free - to be- one with Thee.

Right Choices:

Be rescued today from me, giving it all to Him. When I'm feeling "needy", tell Him and ask for a little relief (see Psalm 22:8).

May 7 – God is Defender

The Bible says, "he restores my soul. He guides me in paths of righteousness for his name's sake. 4Even though I walk through the valley of the shadow of death, I will fear no evil, for you are with me; your rod and your staff, they comfort me" (Psalms 23:3-4).

Defender, who accuses me but Satan and all his evil spirits - legions upon legions they are, but Jesus stands by God to say, all these sins I paid for him/her.

Without God I am:

Defenseless, if only for a moment I could see, the legions of evil spirits that be, screaming in horror they come, silently taking this son.

With God I am:

Defended, sometimes the battle is subtle, one little thought to cuddle, I'm playing with sin deep within, a greater struggle to release it to Him.

Right Choices:

As my mind wonders to the gutter, just stop (see Isaiah 19:20).

MAY 8 – GOD IS OMNIPRESENT

The Bible says, "Where can I go from your Spirit? Where can I flee from your presence? 8If I go up to the heavens, you are there; if I make my bed in the depths, you are there" (Psalms 139:7-8).

Omnipresent, like the air that fills the earth - so is God,
breathe deep His love from above the sod.

Without God I am:

Here, with no fear, I feel no shame in all my fame,
everything is relative to me; my morals are just right to the tee.

With God I am:

There, with a see mark for Heavenly standards - but gone, living this side of eternity with a desire to bring others along.

Right Choices:

Today, Godlike looks like patience, honesty, trust, caring, loving, respecting, caring, giving, and just being nice – smile J (see Jeremiah 23:23,24).

MAY 9 – GOD IS CARING

The Bible says, "Do not be anxious about anything, but in everything, by prayer and petition, with thanksgiving, present your requests to God. 7And the peace of God, which transcends all understanding, will guard your hearts and your minds in Christ Jesus" (Philippians 4:6-7).

Caring, how do we measure His care for us? When things are right we never cuss, He gives to the smallest detail,
so we will not fail or fuss.

Without God I am:

Careless, I burn through people, places and things, no regard for the toil within, soul heavy laden and spirit saddened, I long for my heart to be gladdened.

With God I am:

Careful, when mindful of who I am, to take my stand, this man/woman child shall not depart, from God's Holy plan -
in my heart.

Right Choices:

Care today more about how I honor Christ and all He has done for me – thankful (see 1Timothy 5:4).

MAY 10 – GOD IS INDEPENDENT

The Bible says, "If you fear the LORD and serve and obey him and do not rebel against his commands, and if both you and the king who reigns over you follow the LORD your God--good! 15But if you do not obey the LORD, and if you rebel against his commands, his hand will be against you, as it was against your fathers" (1 Samuel 12: 14-157).

Independent, three in one we've seen the Son, experienced the Spirit, Know the Father's Truth has won, our lives set free to be - saved.

Without God I am:

Dependent, my ability to strive and succeed, to position myself just right, for the fight, I'll take you down - in the first round.

With God I am:

Dependent, on the wholeness of who I am in Him, wanting to be God's man/woman, my perspective extending beyond now, eternally I bow and simply say "wow."

Right Choices:
Free, but a slave to Christ today......no bondage to sin... (see 2 Corinthians 3:17).

MAY 11 – GOD IS OBEDIENT

The Bible says, "For just as through the disobedience of the one man the many were made sinners, so also through the obedience of the one man the many will be made righteous" (Romans 5:19).

Obedient, to His own Word, He does what He says and does not ever break a vow.

Without God I am:

Disobedient, to myself, others and God, I seek a path full of rath, the storm all but the norm, who can see the funnel cloud at night, about to destroy me with all its might.

With God I am:

Disobedient, to myself, others and God, I seek a path full of grace, hope, forgiveness, and mercy, His love will bless - as I confess.

Right Choices:

Obedient to the enabling power of Christ, abiding in the Holy Spirit .....ahh....feel the power.... (see 1Perter 1:2).

May 12 – God is a Servant

The Bible says, "Lord, let your ear be attentive to the prayer of this your servant and to the prayer of your servants who delight in revering your name. Give your servant success today by granting him favor in the presence of this man" (Nehemiah 1:11).

A Servant, knowing our inner most being, He tends to things without our seeing.

Without God I am:

A servant, and a slave to the lusts of the flesh, oh how it feels so fresh.

With God I am:

A servant, to the dominant forces within, God desiring me never to sin, make me a servant Lord of thy will, self desires to kill.

Right Choices:

Whom will the Lord let me serve today as part of His ministry? Be enabled and ready ..... the moment may pass very quickly, but the impact could last a lifetime (see 2 Chronicles 6:16).

May 13 – God is Holy Spirit

The Bible says, "But you will receive power when the Holy Spirit comes on you; and you will be my witnesses in Jerusalem, and in all Judea and Samaria, and to the ends of the earth" (Acts 1:8).

Holy Spirit, one in three, Jesus died on a cross for me,
Father God Holy and pure, knit me together for sure.

Without God I am:

Spirit, filled and led to believe, that by myself, I will weave,
a pattern for my life with meaning, leaning on no one - until it's done.

With God I am:

Spirit, filled and led to believe, that with His help we will weave, a pattern for my life in Him with meaning, leaning on the Son -until it's done.

Right Choices:

Feel the power, hang on ....supercharged on patience, love and a willing spirit (see 1 Thessalonians 4:8).

MAY 14 – GOD IS JESUS CHRIST

The Bible says, "In the beginning was the Word, and the Word was with God, and the Word was God. 2He was with God in the beginning" (John 1:1-2).

Jesus Christ, they formed the heavens together and created me. He came to earth for me to see, a way to go from the foe.

Without God I am:

Condemned, for my sins of past, present and future, but I simply don't get the picture. What have I done to deserve this "gun"?

With God I am:

Redeemed, from my sins of past, present and future, I understand the picture, grace and mercy have come from the Son.

Right Choices:

Never try to understand this, God the Father, God the Son and God the Holy Spirit, the three in one, just believe and experience with faith (see Isaiah 44:6).

MAY 15 – GOD IS REGIMENTED

The Bible says, "Have nothing to do with godless myths and old wives' tales; rather, train yourself to be godly" (1Timothy 4:7).

Regimented, to His unchanging ways, His laws govern all that is perfect for all our days.

Without God I am:

Regimented, and stubborn to a pattern that protects, my life is guarded by what I select.

With God I am:

Regimented, and disciplined mentally to think right thoughts, for this is where the battle is first fought.

Right Choices:

God's laws are perfect, that's why it all works - everyday, the universe hangs together along with billions of souls tending to life - identify today where you are off track, and make it right - do it today (see Judges 2:1-5)!

May 16 – God is Unity

The Bible says, "Hear, O Israel: The Lord our God, the Lord is one. 5Love the Lord your God with all your heart and with all your soul and with all your strength" (Deuteronomy 6:4-5).

Unity, for God is unified in vision and mission, clear in His position, one Theme.

Without God I am:

Unified, with myself and how I view my world and where I fit, all subject to change with one incoming "hit".

With God I am:

Unified, with a sense of assurance, not always sure where I'm going, hang-on to Jesus and keep growing.

Right Choices:

Be open today to the nudges of the Spirit in the quiet places of your self will, letting the Lord draw you near (see Psalm 133:1).

MAY 17 – GOD IS WHOLE

The Bible says, "Wealth and honor come from you; you are the ruler of all things. In your hands are strength and power to exalt and give strength to all" (1Chronicles 29:12).

Whole, the summation of all that is good, all that is lovely, all that is pure, all that is worthy.

Without God I am:

Brokeness, a house created by God, but divided by choices - it will not stand - the test of time.

With God I am:

Wholeness, with Him, I am complete.

Right Choices:

Have a sense today that you lack nothing, but are at a point of maturity in Christ where He would have you - on your way for sure - whole in Him (see Isaiah 54:5).

MAY 18 – GOD IS OMNIPOTENT

The Bible says, "For just as the Father raises the dead and gives them life, even so the Son gives life to whom he is pleased to give it" (John 5:21).

Omnipotent, His purpose and plan accomplished through man, it will not be delayed. He chooses who gets to play.

Without God I am:

Impotent, to be used by God in His way, He desires the final outcome to be swayed - but the choice is mine, to become divine.

With God I am:

Effective, used by God as part - of the great plan, I am used by God in many a heart, thank you Jesus for taking my hand.

Right Choices:

The "cross" was the culmination of His omnipotence, God eternal, Christ -God/man, the perfect lamb, slain for all, and we redeemed, man this is complicated! So, today, just say Lord, I'm yours (see Genesis 17:1).

MAY 19 – GOD IS COURAGE

The Bible says, "For God did not give us a spirit of timidity, but a spirit of power, of love and of self-discipline" (2Timonthy 1:7).

Courage, it must come easy for Him, what can He not do? - whom does He fear? - It must be the "free will" of man, man - unable to stand alone, tempted to sin - it impacts all.

Without God I am:

Courageous, guided by selfish purpose my response is strong, even though it may be wrong.

With God I am:

Courageous, who goes forward? - It is not I alone, for this God has shown, I'm empowered with the Almighty, I'll hold on tightly.

Right Choices:

Courage without Faith is like love without hope. Be faithful with a lot of hope today: you'll be courageous (see Genesis 22:1-14)!

MAY 20 – GOD IS TRIUMPHANT

The Bible says, "Who among the gods is like you, O Lord? Who is like you - majestic in holiness, awesome in glory, working wonders" (Exodus 15:11)?

Triumphant, every hour the Kingdom welcomes thousands of souls into Heaven; what a glorious occasion and joy-filled time, where there is no sin.

Without God I am:

Triumphant, success feels so good, I'm assured now knowing I could, be the best at what I do, this is most important too.

With God I am:

Triumphant, when I love someone in a special way, an encouraging word given today, caring for needs, with loving deeds.

Right Choices:

Be on the winning side of Christ today! Let the wonders of the Lord work within and around what you are doing today (see Hebrews 12:23).

MAY 21 – GOD IS COMPLETE

The Bible says, "For God was pleased to have all his fullness dwell in him, 20and through him to reconcile to himself all things, whether things on earth or things in heaven, by making peace through his blood, shed on the cross" (Colossians 1:19-20).

Complete, they speak of the fullness of God, what can it mean? Sufficient unto its self and not lean, come dwell from this well.

Without God I am:

Incomplete, the hole in this soul, I try to fill - with pills, money, lust, power, pride and selfish will - empty I remain: only Jesus can remove the pain.

With God I am:

Completed, longing in many ways for so many things, I struggle to be content with what He brings, look more carefully at all I am - what a bounty of a man/woman.

Right Choices:

Remember, God doesn't make junk and his plan is perfect, you are where you are and God thinks you are pretty neat (see Mark 12:30)!

May 22 – God is Great

The Bible says, "The LORD is slow to anger and great in power; the LORD will not leave the guilty unpunished. His way is in the whirlwind and the storm, and clouds are the dust of his feet" (Nahum 1:3).

Great, when we look at the history of man, we see turmoil, strife and pain, was this God's aim? - who is to blame, but all our shame. This God is great, it's not too late to seek a new fate.

Without God I am:

Great, my path seems sure, money is one lure, not bad in itself, but it can medicate my health, before God in how I handle wealth.

With God I am:

Great, wanting motives to be pure, I keep God in sight for sure, seeking to be my best, knowing I'll be blest.

Right Choices:

Such a small word for such a "great" God, be big today in Him (see 2 Chronicles 2:5)!

May 23 – God is Leading

The Bible says, "Submit to God and be at peace with him; in this way prosperity will come to you" (Job 22:21).

Leading, like a lighthouse on a dark stormy sea at night, He beckons me to give up the fight, steer clear of dangerous rocks. He guides our lives to a Heavenly dock.

Without God I am:

Leading, my life and all that matters, while choirs of Angels become sadder, the further I go - the more distant I become, turn now and receive the Son.

With God I am:

Following, a God who seems distant at times, it was I who turned away to find, some other god pleasing thing, feeding my sin, I turn to see Him, near and dear, loving me within.

Right Choices:

Put self second today behind an almighty God, and see where He leads....it will be to a good place (see Romans 5:21).

MAY 24 – GOD IS GRANTING

The Bible says, "Jabez cried out to the God of Israel, "Oh, that you would bless me and enlarge my territory! Let your hand be with me, and keep me from harm so that I will be free from pain." And God granted his request" (1Chronicles 4:10).

Granting, of true penitence for our ugly and mean sins placed at the foot of the cross - now vanished with Him, strengthened by His Spirit, living as we ought, my tempestuous will is taught.

Without God I am:

Granted, to have a free will to choose, who will be god (God) of this life to loose, giving it to Him or me, my mind needs renewal to see.

With God I am:

Granted, the mystery of new life, bondage clings to the sin within, oh to let it go and abide with Him, I've grown accustomed to the stench of this sweet sin.

Right Choices:

It's my turn today to be a grantor to God, surrendering my will, so that He can fill (see Proverbs 8:21).

May 25 – God is Valuable

The Bible says, "Now if you obey me fully and keep my covenant, then out of all nations you will be my treasured possession. Although the whole earth is mine, 6you will be for me a kingdom of priests and a holy nation.' These are the words you are to speak to the Israelites" (Exodus 19:5-6).

Valuable, in ways we barely understand, how do we measure joy? How do we measure peace? He chose us and has a plan, listen carefully to Him as He whispers it to you.

Without God I am:

Valued, by God in the same way as those who believe,
used by God in ways to work the plan, stop-look and listen, what you fear you will lose, is not worth keeping.

With God I am:

Valued, by God for the richness of my heart, mind, soul and spirit, God looks at me and sees His Son, not my sin – Yes, Lord rest deep within - direct my thoughts to your joyful presence.

Right Choices:

Yes, but for a whiff of time, but oh what a precious whiff (see 2 Chronicles 2:16).

May 26 – God is with Me

The Bible says, "The LORD himself goes before you and will be with you; he will never leave you nor forsake you. Do not be afraid; do not be discouraged" (Deuteronomy 31:8).

With me, what a gift indeed, I didn't earn it, can't work to keep it, God will never take it away or leave me, He's with me through eternity - Amen!

Without God I am:

Whoever's, but mostly mine, I deserve myself for this is what I worship, my self will - passions and desires screaming to be fed, fat with deceit, I've normalized my sin - I'm fine.

With God I am:

His, died to self – oh, what can this mean? Jesus' love flowing within, my only true desire to be near Him, He enables, directs, leads, guides, assures, encourages me to where and what I must be.

Right Choices:

Let this little part of God in me today become just a little bit bigger (see Deuteronomy 7:9).

May 27 – God is a Messenger

The Bible says, ""See, I will send my messenger, who will prepare the way before me. Then suddenly the Lord you are seeking will come to his temple; the messenger of the covenant, whom you desire, will come," says the
LORD Almighty." (Malachi 3:1).

A messenger, speaking through His Holy Word, revealed in creation and evangelized by believers with His Holy Spirit, a Living force that beckons us to Him.

Without God I am:

A message, my life, my actions, my words, my thoughts all recorded for review at destinies gate, judgment is sure to come.

With God I am:

A message, of an Almighty God who gave me a renewed spirit to enable my fallen evil self to make a better choice, choosing life, not death or sin, forgiven and repenting - my desires change within.

Right Choices:

My message starts with how I think, more than what I say, followed by what I do - be mindful of Him today (see Matthew 11:1).

MAY 28 – GOD IS CALLING

The Bible says, "How great is the love the Father has lavished on us, that we should be called children of God! And that is what we are! The reason the world does not know us is that it did not know him" (1John 3:1).

Calling us to accept our very own nature, treating it charitably, firmly, and intelligently. We are the product of our circumstances, listen to God quietly, and accept His joy as a gift.

Without God I am:

Called, to view this instant in time as my nature, my lot in life as my own conquest and vanity, we dare to be
happy at all expense.

With God I am:

Called, by God to humble myself and pray for Him to deposit in my soul true joy, for in no way can I be the author of lasting peace unto myself.

Right Choices:

So many voices calling to me today, the worry and anxiety deafen my ears to the calm assuring love of the Lord (see Mark 15:3).

MAY 29 – GOD IS CHANGING US

The Bible says, "My dear children, I write this to you so that you will not sin. But if anybody does sin, we have one who speaks to the Father in our defense-- Jesus Christ, the Righteous One. 2He is the atoning sacrifice for our sins,
and not only for ours but also for All the sins of the whole world" (1John 2:1-2).

Changing us, each day as we cast the obedient wills of our lives on His throne, our desire becomes to be His - as He
deposits His love and nurtures our soul.

Without God I am:

Changed, by the disease and evil that lurks within, it pulls me deeper and deeper until it has my very soul.

With God I am:

Changed, by the grace and redeeming love of God,
to live a new life.

Right Choices:

How many of us would like another year just like the one we had? Well, parts of it were good for sure, but the adventure of each new day brings opportunity - for change (see James 1:17).

MAY 30 – GOD IS SAVING US

The Bible says, "he saved us, not because of righteous things we had done, but because of his mercy. He saved us through the washing of rebirth and renewal by the Holy Spirit" (Titus 3:5).

He is saving us, from eternal separation from Him and an eternity of agony, terror, and horrific gloom; to a redeemed eternal life in paradise, doing His work.

Without God I am:

Deceived, in my mind to think I can be my own god, I'm always more important than others and I can take care of myself - always - forever.

With God I am:

Saved, from my own fallen self, the original nature that knows so much ugliness and meanness; to a redeemed life of second chances.

Right Choices:

Saved for sure, but savor the "saving", for sanctification brings endorphins to the soul for renewed energy - taking us to a higher place - closer to God (see Hebrews 11:7).

May 31 – God is Tending To Us

The Bible says, "Let us fix our eyes on Jesus, the author and perfecter of our faith, who for the joy set before him endured the cross, scorning its shame, and sat down at the right hand of the throne of God" (Hebrews 12:2).

Tending to us, by His word, His Angels and others who He chooses to minister to our every need, night and day.

Without God I am:

Tending to me, but I set my limits to show that I am good, better than most, caring as needed to the few I choose, now it's time to get on with me.

With God I am:

Tending to my spirit by reading His word daily, praying, praising Him, and loving others by kind words, and actions.

Right Choices:

Whatever I may have done that is causing grief matters not, once I turn it over to Him, to be tended in His loving way (see James 3:17).

June 1 – God is Ministering to Us

The Bible says, "He makes winds his messengers, flames of fire his servants" (Psalm 104:4).

Ministering to us, in ways we barely understand, a time for solace and reflection, time for growing courage and strength, He's feeding my soul through His Holy Spirit, my heart and mind rejoice.

Without God I am:

Ministered to, by forces and powers I barely understand, my strong will and evil spirits who want my deceived soul to keep full - of lies.

With God I am:

Ministered to, by angels sent from the throne of God, caring for and protecting me from danger, laying a path and guiding my heart and mind with a nourished spirit and soul.

Right Choices:

Hold loosely to the things of this world, butt naked I came in, and butt naked I'll go out. Embrace today what He gives, and let go what He takes away (see Hebrews 1:14).

June 2 – God is Reconciling Us

The Bible says, "All this is from God, who reconciled us to himself through Christ and gave us the ministry of reconciliation" (2 Corinthians 5:18).

Reconciling us, Satan stands at the throne of God accusing us of our sins, but Jesus is seated at the right hand of God claiming victory over our sin and owning us as one of His.

Without God I am:

Reconciled to, a life for some which on the surface appears enviable, for others a life of bitterness and resentment, and for others, lazy bliss where my life is my tomb and grave.

With God I am:

Reconciled, to a Heavenly Father whose love and acceptance are endless, so great that He gave His one and only Son, just for me.

Right Choices:

Let the accuser have no case about me today, I never thought about how my sin saddens God, until I realized how much he paid with His life and blood for my soul (see Revalations12:10).

JUNE 3 – GOD IS LISTENING

The Bible says, "We know that God does not listen to sinners. He listens to the godly man who does his will (John 9:31).

Listening, to the world and all our selfish pride, Lord please give us a free ride, but God says no - it's time to grow, give your will over and let me flow so you can sow.

Without God I am:

Listening, to the heartbeat and rhythm of the world, I plan my moves and set the stage not realizing how strong I've built my cage.

With God I am:

Listening, to that sweet quiet whisper of God, encouraging me on to be strong, an obedient will fills a sacred heart, I'm one with Him ready to win.

Right Choices:

My normal hearing is not what it used to be, the hearing aids help, but what really tunes me into God is another's happy heart, the smile on a child's face, the loving touch of my wife. Look today and listen for the tender touch of God (see Proverbs 28:14).

June 4 – God is Watching

The Bible says, "from his dwelling place he watches all who live on earth" (Psalm 33:14).

Watching, not from a distance, but near and dear, He looks deep within, looking for Him, wanting to see at the core of our desire, a passion for Him of fire.

Without God I am:

Watching, the dashboard of my life, my happiness, health, wealth, fame and friends - family, usually in that order, my spirit is growing poorer.

With God I am:

Watching, the Lord work within, I've given over control to Him, guide me, shape me, mold me, yes Lord, yes Lord, yes Lord.

Right Choices:

It's ok that He's watching, don't fret over it, the good news is He cares. Free up, give it up, abide, let go of the anxiety, fear of this world - soak your soul in surrender (see Proverbs 2:8).

June 5 – God is Fullness

The Bible says, "..and I pray that…you may have power, together with all the saints, to grasp how wide and long and high and deep is the love of Christ, 19and to know this love that surpasses knowledge--that you may be filled to the measure of all the fullness of God" (Ephesians 3:18-19).

Fullness, In our daily striving we seek to add food, health, wealth, power and sometimes understanding, but rarely seek it from Him, He holds it all in His open hand, freely He gives.

Without God I am:

Empty, striving to be something I need more of, it never seems enough, like a junkie I need a higher hit, let me cram some bit more into this empty hole of life.

With God I am:

Filled, with the immediate presence and power of Christ, I'm competent to cope, courageous to become, confident in the renewal of my mind to see and go, doing His will.

Right Choices:

My thoughts today drive me to places where I shouldn't go, remember how vast and immense is the span of God's control - let it go, cling to Him (see 1Peter 4:7).

June 6 – God is Pardoning Us

The Bible says, "Let the wicked forsake his way and the evil man his thoughts. Let him turn to the LORD, and he will have mercy on him, and to our God, for he will freely pardon" (Isaiah 55:7).

Pardoning us, as we humbly confess and repent of wrongful thoughts, words and actions, His love and forgiveness floats us on the sea of life, upholding us with a lasting grace.

Without God I am:

Excused, by myself for having explained, I put all those things of wrong in a nice compartment or wear it as a prideful attitude. I have no shame, and it's just the way we are - look around.

With God I am:

Pardoned, left with the consequences of my sin, but restored in a relationship - my soul clings to God, my character renewed.

Right Choices:

The mystery of God, my life and redemption is deep water. God knows I can't do it, but I don't (see Psalm 25:11)

JUNE 7 – GOD IS A PIT STOP

The Bible says, "Come to me, all you who are weary and burdened, and I will give you rest. 29Take my yoke upon you and learn from me, for I am gentle and humble in heart, and you will find rest for your souls. 30For my yoke
is easy and my burden is light." (Matthew 11:28-30).

A pit stop, where I race with an empty weary soul to a place of refuge and filling up, God, however, wants to be my daily companion, minute by minute feeding my soul, keeping it full.

Without God I am:

Fueled, by the jazz of my freedom in self, to do as I please,
to wherever I please, Satan opens the door wide, I am on his side, what a slide.

With God I am:

Fueled, by the love of a very giving and forgiving God,
my meager ways so often forget Him, yet He is near and dear within.

Right Choices:

It's truer than you think! Yeah, life is crazy, and this power turn I just screamed through burned my tires, emptied my tank; filler up Jesus and renew my spirit (see 2 Samuel 22:33)!

June 8 – God is Amazing

The Bible says, "He got up, took his mat and walked out in full view of them all. This amazed everyone and they praised God, saying, "We have never seen anything like this!" (Mark 2:12).

Amazing, He healed the sick, made the blind see, enabled the lame to walk, put the stars in their place, and created man in His own image.

Without God I am:

Amazed, that if there is a God that He lets me get away with what I do.

With God I am:

Amazed, that He is slow to anger, patient with me to learn, wanting that none should perish and be lost, He longs for me to sow - His word among the foe.

Right Choices:

No one has ever seen Him, but yet we all have experienced Him. Glimpse's of creation, the miracle of life, freedom from guilt, enabling love, a tender heart, but above all - the wonder of His Son and how He won - the battle once for all - so, go in tow (see Revelations 15:3)!

June 9 – God is Here

The Bible says, "The LORD is near to all who call on him, to all who call on him in truth. 19He fulfills the desires of those who fear him; he hears their cry and saves them. 20The LORD watches over all who love him, but all the wicked he will destroy" (Psalms 145:18-20).

Here, in the midst of our busy lives we fill the space where God is with so many things that we crowd Him out, no room at this inn, yet He clings.

Without God I am:

Filled, with ignorant desire and blind faith, my passions seek a path well-traveled by the world around me.

With God I am:

Filled, with awe and wonder of this Almighty God, I stumble along, oh to grab hold, and be bold, to let His life flow, through my soul.

Right Choices:

Wherever I go, there I am, and the good news is, He is too. Don't feel alone today, because we are not (see Jude 1:24)!

JUNE 10 – GOD IS AMBITIOUS

The Bible says, "For since death came through a man, the resurrection of the dead comes also through a man. 22For as in Adam all die, so in Christ all will be made alive" (1 Corinthians 15: 21-22).

Ambitious, daily God tends to billions and billions of lives, millions of prayers, tens of thousands deaths, tens of thousands of births. His network is perfect, never overloaded, never down, His focus remains on each one alone.

Without God I am:

Ambitious, to live my life along a common path, seeking to build assurance from my wealth, I wonder why I prosper. God is not in it, but yet He is in ways I don't understand.

With God I am:

Ambitious, driven by hope, faith and love, I smile at each new day, ready to play, taking seriously what God has planned for me today.

Right Choices:

While my energy level has it's up's and down's, ambition is fueled from another place - namely passion and vision, so be a visionary today (see Numbers 24:4).

JUNE 11 – GOD IS CHANGING OUR DESIRES

The Bible says, "Create in me a pure heart, O God, and renew a steadfast spirit within me. 11Do not cast me from your presence or take your Holy Spirit from me. 12Restore to me the joy of your salvation and grant me a willing spirit, to sustain me" (Psalms 51:10-12).

Changing our desires, with each mindful thought of who God is and how wonderful His love for us really is.

Without God I am:

Fat, dumb and happy, in the midst of all my selfish pride, arrogance and spiteful rage.

With God I am:

Slow to learn, but yet learning, directionally correct, this God is patient with me, eternity is a long time. Best I keep my passions contained with a perspective of everlasting purpose.

Right Choices:

Be careful what I desire today, as we think, so we go (see Job 23:13).

JUNE 12 – GOD IS GRIEVED

The Bible says, "I am afraid that when I come again my God will humble me before you, and I will be grieved over many who have sinned earlier and have not repented of the impurity, sexual sin and debauchery in which they have indulged" (2Corinthians 12:21).

Grieved, by our stubborn wills that choose out of godly neglect, sinful ways, yet we are still blest.

Without God I am:

"Out to lunch", no one is tending this soul, yet the evil forces that bid it low, are guiding me to Sheol.

With God I am:

Attacked, by Satan, who is passionate and focused on ruining the lives of God's chosen ones. Evil forces spare no mercy, I submit by choice, deceived by wrong thinking.

Right Choices:

First deceived, now grieved, it's like the pain that heals the soul, part of His plan to make me God's man, woman, child whole (see 1Peter 1:6).

June 13 – God is Touching Our Lives

The Bible says, "I will put my dwelling place among you, and I will not abhor you. 12I will walk among you and be your God, and you will be my people" (Leviticus 26:11-12).

Touching our lives, as our hearts become more tender, and our minds become more mindful, of this Almighty God and His abounding Grace, Mercy and Love.

Without God I am:

Touched, by the lives of some very wonderful people, I stand in awe of their simple faith and wonder how can it be?

With God I am:

Touched, by the compassion of God, I feel His peace and assurance of His care over my life now and through eternity - how beautiful!

Right Choices:

Touch, the sense that assures, look for the areas in my life today that are being "touched" by the hand of God (see Psalm 103:13).

June 14 – God is Amending

The Bible says, "Fools mock at making amends for sin, but goodwill is found among the upright" (Proverbs 14:9).

Amending, the broken-hearted hurt in our lives from past afflictions, His healing touch mends emotional scars, creating a redeemed self – strengthened.

Without God I am:

Amended, and confused to a state of despair from all my wrong choices, I am what I am, there seems no escape.

With God I am:

Amended, by God as I yield my will to His will, I desire more of what He is, and less of who I was.

Right Choices:

Try today not to undo what God has made right. Try, such a small word for such a large task, but it gets bigger and easier when we add surrender (see - Jeremiah 35:15).

June 15 – God is a Shelter

The Bible says, "I long to dwell in your tent forever and take refuge in the shelter of your wings" (Psalms 61:4).

A shelter, protecting us from evil and harm, if we make the Lord our refuge, run here when sin knocks, He's our rock.

Without God I am:

Not able to run or hide, from the evil that stalks my soul, or the Love of God who wants to call this heart home.

With God I am:

Sheltered, if I choose to seek His refuge, no temptation is so great that God cannot keep me from it, if I seek His shelter.

Right Choices:

When I go into a shelter, what am I doing? Am I not inside something or under something? So, what does it mean to be under or inside God - think about this today (see Revelation 7:15)?

June 16 – God is a Calming Us

The Bible says, "He got up, rebuked the wind and said to the waves, "Quiet! Be still!" Then the wind died down and it was completely calm" (Mark 4:39).

Calming us, while anxiety rages through our bodies, we pray, and instantly we feel the cool shade of this Almighty
God take our hand.

Without God I am:

Anxious, about the future, my life, what may happen,
potential results that drive fear very near.

With God I am:

Calmed, by the presence of an Almighty God, who will not
let one minute detail of my life be left to chance.

Right Choices:

Calmed with a peace that passes all understanding, because I choose wisely, to be more concerned about who I am in Christ than what I am in the world (see Proverbs 17:27).

June 17 – God is a Teaching Us

The Bible says, "They were amazed at his teaching, because his message had authority" (Luke 4:32).

Teaching us, about His nature, immensity and power, He wants us to make right choices, first in how we think, then what we say, and finally what we do.

Without God I am:

Taught, all too often all the wrong things, by where my ears go, what my eyes see, how my mind thinks and my heart feels.

With God I am:

Taught, that no temptation is so great that God cannot provide a way out for me.

Right Choices:

Teaching implies I am learning and moving onto to new levels of understanding, crave knowledge from the Teacher and draw near (see 1 Corinthians 10:13).

June 18 – God is Cleansing Us

The Bible says, "And the peace of God, which transcends all understanding, will guard your hearts and your minds in Christ Jesus" (Philippians 4:7).

Cleansing us, as His love and abiding Spirit partakes of our life, desires change and a peace that passes all understanding abides.

Without God I am:

Contaminated, by the evil of the world and fallen people who all have one aim, to prosper self and serve passions.

With God I am:

Cleansed, white as snow, no sin or wrong is too big for this awesome God, yield it over to Him, let the bondage go - daily.

Right Choices:

It's hard to live and not get dirty, especially if you are pushing life with your pedal to the metal, natural man becoming a saint. So, remember today to use some soap on the soul, by asking Him for forgiveness and being thankful (see Proverbs 30:12).

June 19 – God is Keeping Me from Myself

The Bible says, "For where you have envy and selfish ambition, there you find disorder and every evil practice" (James 3:16).

Keeping me from myself, which I hate to let Him do, we love our sin and don't want to let it go, we feel entitled to indulge, "give me a fix now - oh yes - self" - but God says no.

Without God I am:

Indulged in self, for what else matters, I'm god of this life, yesterday is past, tomorrow may never come, only today counts.

With God I am:

Indulged in battle, of wills - mine or God's, why is it so hard? Why can it not be clearer? God can't drive a parked car, so I keep my wheels moving, my heart praying.

Right Choices:

This is big! At the end of the day and end of my life, how I dealt with me will be the key, for nothing good exists in me aside from the grace of God (see James 5:5).

June 20 – God is Restoring Us

The Bible says, "So he went down and dipped himself in the Jordan seven times, as the man of God had told him, and his flesh was restored and became clean like that of a young boy" (2Kings 5:14).

Restoring us, to a life with Him, both for now and in eternity, we slowly begin to see, how miserable our life is with only me, and not Him.

Without God I am:

Broken, by the hurt and rejection of friends, I feel no assurance in any relationships. Yet I run and seek new ones daily to feed my longing empty heart.

With God I am:

Restored, and made new, purer are my thoughts, a more wholesome life I lead, His grace, mercy, and love make me feel accepted from above.

Right Choices:

Restoration is hard work and we soon discover the old surfaces of sin peel away slowly, but surely with the cleansing blood of Christ (see Zephaniah 3:9).

June 21 – God is Helping Us

The Bible says, "I will exalt you, O LORD, for you lifted me out of the depths and did not let my enemies gloat over me. 2O LORD my God, I called to you for help and you healed me. 3O LORD, you brought me up from the grave; you spared me from going down into the pit" (Psalms 30:1-3).

Helping us, to be more of what He wants us to be, focused more on who we are, not what we are.

Without God I am:

Helped, by the results of actions taken, sinking deeper into the consequences of life's choices, oh so many voices, if only I had it to do over again.

With God I am:

Helped, to be beyond me.

Right Choices:

Yes, helping for sure, but the real key here is more letting Him do the doing. It does not come naturally for any of us. The help is our conscious effort to be open (see 1Corinthians 12:28).

June 22 – God is Pruning Us

The Bible says, "He cuts off every branch in me that bears no fruit, while every branch that does bear fruit he prunes so that it will be even more fruitful" (John 15:2).

Pruning us, of the branches in our lives that are diseased and robbing us of being fruit-bearing in our lives.

Without God I am:

Growing wild, in all directions, my life seems out of control, too many distractions, dead-end streets, endless energy-yielding so little contentment.

With God I am:

Groomed, with a sense of priorities, knowing which efforts bear fruit, this tree is healthy, fed by the streams of God's living water.

Right Choices:

When I'm pruning my fruit trees, a good friend once said, "you just have to eliminate the confusion". So, as I looked at the tree, any branch that didn't seem to have a clear purpose would be cut off. So it is with the parts of my life that the Lord feels lack purpose for His plan (see Isaiah 18:5).

June 23 – God is Bread

The Bible says, "Then Jesus declared, "I am the bread of life. He who comes to me will never go hungry, and he who believes in me will never be thirsty" (John 6:35).

Bread, of life who sustains us, blessing us with what we need, not deserve.

Without God I am:

Fed, on the adrenaline of a higher fix, a more impassioned dare, how far will I go and who will care.

With God I am:

Filled, daily as I take time with Him, to pray, reflect on His goodness and my pride and selfishness, His love for me and His desire for me to see Him.

Right Choices:

Bread brings life to the body and is needed regularly, just like our need to draw near the Lord daily for strength (see John 6:33).

June 24 – God is Quieting Us

The Bible says, "But I have stilled and quieted my soul; like a weaned child with its mother, like a weaned child is my soul within me" (Psalm 131:2).

Quieting us, with quiet assurance of His presence, the force that He holds in His hand, the great plan.

Without God I am:

Restless, and anxious at times, looking intently for the right signs, I push and shove and scheme, "where is my dream" - I scream.

With God I am:

Quieted, with the assurance of the closeness of His guidance. I walk on in the shadow of the glory and grace of Almighty God.

Right Choices:

Quieted by the immensity of an all-powerful God whose love is immeasurable (see Psalm 23:2)!

JUNE 25 – GOD IS INSTRUCTING US

The Bible says, "It was good for me to be afflicted so that I might learn your decrees" (Psalm 119:71).

Instructing us, as we give over our minds and wills, letting Him fill, our hearts with the knowledge of Him deep within.

Without God I am:

Instructed, by my learned mind and passion-filled desires, seeking to make a living, I honestly pursue my dreams, "is this all there is?"- I ask.

With God I am:

Instructed, as I choose to act in small steps of obedience, an amazing blessing of a divine peace comes, teaching me.

Right Choices:

God's instruction manual for life, the Bible. Be sure to read it today and seek its instruction and learning (see Joshua 1:18).

June 26 – God is Purifying Us

The Bible says, "Dear friends, this is now my second letter to you. I have written both of them as reminders to stimulate you to wholesome thinking" (2Peter 3:1).

Purifying us, from the filth of wrongful thoughts, selfish pride and sinful acts.

Without God I am:

Contaminated, with the wrongful ways of the world, what do I see and what do I think, write down my thoughts for a day and see, let a friend read it to me.

With God I am:

Purified, moment by moment as the living waters of Christ enlighten me, why is the cesspool of sin so inviting, somehow it delights, but for a moment.

Right Choices:

What happens when something becomes more pure? Does it not only begin to take on the "original" look, so it is with man, before the fall (see James 4:8).

June 27 – God is Immortal Hope

The Bible says, "In the way of righteousness there is life; along that path is immortality" (Proverbs 12:28).

Immortal hope, He is wanting that none would perish to damnation. He admonishes all to share His light, have faith, hope and love, and the greatest of these is love.

Without God I am:

Immortal, destined for eternal conscious awareness of my doomed deep despair, the rage of my cage in me - total agony.

With God I am:

Immortal, destined for eternal glory with Christ, my conscious awareness is filled with worshiping and serving this Heavenly King.

Right Choices:

Realizing that our glory with Christ is eternal and we will be immortal, take the long view of life and its true purpose today and the value it truly has for a child of God (see Psalm 37:34).

June 28 – God is With Us

The Bible says, "What, then, shall we say in response to this? If God is for us, who can be against us" (Romans 8:31)?

With us, now for a time, will I choose to let Him be mine, for all time.

Without God I am:

Not alone, for the Devil and all his evil spirits guide my path, most of the time it has little wrath, unsuspecting, I walk on, could this be all wrong?

With God I am:

Not alone, for an Almighty God has hold of my ear, I have no fear, for He is near.

Right Choices:

The good news and bad news story, we don't always get it right, but transparency has no equal with God - He knows it all, whether we like it or not. So, be transparent with Him today, telling it like it is (see Luke 11:17)

June 29 – God is Reconciling Us

The Bible says, "that God was reconciling the world to himself in Christ, not counting men's sins against them. And he has committed to us the message of reconciliation" (2 Corinthians 5:19).

Reconciling us from sorrow, the loss of a loved one, grieved with the affliction of a serious disease, God works to meet every emotional and physical need.

Without God I am:

Stuffed with sorrow, the clutter and fullness of this room bulges at the seams, my eyes mirror my heavy heart.

With God I am:

Reconciled, and set free, it's not just mental, it's emotional, physical and spiritual - this is real stuff, I know God is real because I feel His presence.

Right Choices:

Reconciling is a good thing, but oh what a price! Treasure the payment made, keep it clean, protect it and be good (see Colossians 1:20).

June 30 – God is Giving Our Lives Meaning

The Bible says, "and if you call out for insight and cry aloud for understanding, 4and if you look for it as for silver and search for it as for hidden treasure, 5then you will understand the fear of the LORD and find the knowledge of God. 6For the LORD gives wisdom, and from his mouth come knowledge and understanding" (Proverbs 2:3-6).

Giving our lives meaning, in each moment as we look and
see how He uses me, we sense His presence and feel blessed,
to be part of this mess.

Without God I am:

Giving myself meaning, with the ritual of my days, if only
I could see the walls I've built around my ways - a living tomb.

With God I am:

Filled with purpose, I sometimes stray, but then I pray, thank you God - my guide, don't let me hide.

Right Choices:

My significance today is who I am in Christ (see John 20:31).

July 1– God is Pardoning Us

The Bible says, "Let the wicked forsake his way and the evil man his thoughts. Let him turn to the LORD, and he will have mercy on him, and to our God, for he will freely pardon" (Isaiah 55:7).

Pardoning us, as we seek Him, asking for forgiveness and repenting of our sin, for no wrong, is too great and it's never too late, while yet we live.

Without God I am:

Prejudiced, to believe that this sin I take and keep in my life is a greater joy and finer partner then the redeeming Love of a Savior.

With God I am:

Pardoned, set free from the prison gates and bondage of my sin, I seek to think better thoughts and act in ways that honor Him.

Right Choices:

Pardoning is an act of forgiveness, as I have been, so I will also pardon (see Micah 7:18).

July 2 – God is Relieving Us

The Bible says, ""Be still, and know that I am God; I will be exalted among the nations, I will be exalted in the earth." 11The LORD Almighty is with us; the God of Jacob is our fortress" (Psalms 46:10-11).

Relieving us, from the guilt and shame of past sins, He's
taking my anxious thoughts about today and tomorrow,
and loving me - helping me to be whole.

Without God I am:

Relieved, only as time passes and I see the dreadful outcome I hoped would not happen has passed me by, could this be God's Grace staring me in the face?

With God I am:

Relieved, in knowing the depth of the love of this God for me, I praise Him on bended knee.

Right Choices:

Relieving us, meaning to remove (a person) from pain, discomfort and or anxiety - so I, will be today (see Psalm 4:1).

July 3 – God is Life to the Mind - Renewal

The Bible says, "Do not conform any longer to the pattern of this world, but be transformed by the renewing of your mind. Then you will be able to test and approve what God's will is--his good, pleasing and perfect will" (Romans 12:2).

Life to the mind - Renewal, as He breathes His purpose to my yearning soul, seeking Him - my thoughts are renewed, we have a clear perspective of the world.

Without God I am:

Filled with wrong thinking, for what do I see and how do I think when I gaze upon the world, my city or my street, write down my thoughts - share it with a pastor.

With God I am:

Filled with more good thinking, for the mind is the roadway of my life, so as I think, there will I go.

Right Choices:

You know you are getting close to God when you begin to become more thrilled with the oneness of Christ than the oneness of self (see Titus 3:5).

July 4 – God is Health for the Body

The Bible says, "My son, pay attention to what I say; listen closely to my words. 21Do not let them out of your sight, keep them within your heart; 22for they are life to those who find them and health to a man's whole body" (Proverbs 4:20-22).

Health for the body, for He relaxes my tensions, gives peace to my mind, and fills me with love divine, I feel fine.

Without God I am:

At risk, of letting my actions have deadly effect on my body. I do things for short term relief because my belief is caged in sin, deep within - anger, bitterness, and resentment.

With God I am:

At ease, with the presence of God, He fills a vacant place in my heart, I tried to fill it with other stuff, but my life became rough.

Right Choices:

Illness consumes our mind when our body is afflicted, be intentional about inflicting wellness with the right food, exercise, for the body is the temple of God (see 3 John 1:2).

July 5 – God is Mine

The Bible says, "My flesh and my heart may fail, but God is the strength of my heart and my portion forever" (Psalms 74:26).

Mine, to have and to hold today and forever, at first because of selfish need and knowing what's right for me, but as I grow He enables me to sow - His word and Love.

Without God I am:

Mine, only and alone, I believe, this is a scary place to be, think about it!

With God I am:

Mine, to be what God would have me be, in thought, word and deed, free to choose, and more and more to lose hold of myself.

Right Choices:

My right to myself is the most important thing I can give to Christ (see Psalm 119:36).

July 6 – God is Sufficient

The Bible says, "But he said to me, "My grace is sufficient for you, for my power is made perfect in weakness." Therefore I will boast all the more gladly about my weaknesses, so that Christ's power may rest on me" (2Corinthians 12:9".

Sufficient, for me and all my needs, He opens and closes doors of opportunity, He directs my steps, and we only need to say "I can - with His help".

Without God I am:

Sufficient, to believe in error that my capable talents are all that I need, for some it seems to work, many even prosper.

With God I am:

Sufficient, in the oneness with Christ, He's my companion, my confidence, courage, and strength.

Right Choices:

What can fill this craving for more worldly "stuff", but the sufficiency and fullness of Christ (see 2 Corinthians 12:9)?

July 7 – God is Angry

The Bible says, "Who is a God like you, who pardons sin and forgives the transgression of the remnant of his inheritance? You do not stay angry forever but delight to show mercy" (Micah 7:18).

Angry, when we knowingly choose to turn our back on Him and sin, how numb and dumb can we be, was it really selfish pride, some sickness deep inside, Jesus says, Pray - and I will give you strength.

Without God I am:

Angry, at the consequences of "things" that just seem to happen, my bitterness and resentment consume me, how did these things happen to me? I feel abused and used by the greed of people.

With God I am:

Angry, at myself for bad choices made, I know God has heard my prayers and forgiven me, but now I must forgive myself, as God has done, He has more important things for me to do.

Right Choices:

Don't ever be in the path of God's anger or the cause of it (see Numbers 14:16).

JULY 8 – GOD IS HAPPY

The Bible says, ""His master replied, 'Well done, good and faithful servant! You have been faithful with a few things; I will put you in charge of many things. Come and share your master's happiness'" (Matthew 25:23)!

Happy, when we turn to Him in humbleness, seeking restoration in relationship - daily, He hates our sin, but still, He loves us, He gives us what we need, not deserve.

Without God I am:

Happy, in my own way, for now as I play, at feeding my whims, careful always to win.

With God I am:

Happy, in knowing that my circumstances go beyond this life, which is filled with stress, worry, and emotional - physical strife. Jesus says His yoke is light. I must keep Him in my sight.

Right Choices:

It is better to let it happen for the right reasons than seek it for the wrong ones (see 1 Chronicles 16:31).

July 9 – God is Listening

The Bible says, "Before a word is on my tongue you know it completely, O LORD" (Psalm 139:4).

Listening, He is to the heartbeat of my inner soul, looking at intent, motivation, desire, longing and passion. He understands my deepest need, so He can feed this hungry soul.

Without God I am:

Listening, and watching for the threats that come my way, to derail my sleigh, lookout, or you will pay.

With God I am:

Listening, to God's whispers to me, you see I want to be, all that He desires for me. I'm afraid I'm growing deaf if only He would "yell"! - Maybe He is?

Right Choices:

Well, Satan whispers too, sometimes louder and more clearly, so, if you could smell it, it would stink. Think about the smell and looking like it (see 2 Timothy 4:4).

July 10 – God is Refreshing Us

The Bible says, "Repent, then, and turn to God, so that your sins may be wiped out, that times of refreshing may come from the Lord" (Acts 3:19).

Refreshing us, like the incoming tide that flushes over a mucky hot smelly beach, so too do the living waters
of Christ cleanse me.

Without God I am:

Refreshed, for a moment like putting deodorant on my hot sweating armpits, it smells good for a while.

With God I am:

Refreshed, when I choose to take time for Him, reading His word, praying, calling to encourage a friend or sending
and email to say "hi" and pass along a good thought.

Right Choices:

Getting cleaned up and refreshed always means getting rid of something, usually by a change in environment - Maui, a nice refreshing shower on a hot day, cold glass of mint water, laughter with friends, let the Lord smile on you today (see Acts 3:20).

July 11– God is Easy

The Bible says, "For my yoke is easy and my burden is light." (Matthew 11:30).

Easy, He is to understand, difficult to fathom, impossible to contain.

Without God I am:

Easily, led astray down a path which is wide.

With God I am:

Easily, led along a narrow road with boundaries.

Right Choices:

An old oxen yoke hangs in my garage from the farm I grew up on, it weighs about 150 lbs. It bears the Bible verse mentioned here, but God says my burden is light, that's because He's carrying it, let Him carry you today and keep you on the narrow path (see Matthew 7:13).

JULY 12– GOD IS INSPIRING US

The Bible says, "All Scripture is God-breathed and is useful for teaching, rebuking, correcting and training in righteousness, 17so that the man of God may be thoroughly equipped for every good work" (2Timothy 3:16-17).

Inspiring us, as we pause and reflect on His word and creation.

Without God I am:

Inspired, to drink the sweet smells of sin, because this is what my body and mind want.

With God I am:

Inspired, to think about what I'm doing, the consequences for dear ones close to me, including my relationship with Christ.

Right Choices:

I'm trusting that God is as inspiring to you as He has been to me with these daily devotions. Yes, mere words, but living truth and power directly from the indwelling Holy Spirit, within you and me (see 1 Thessalonians 1:3)

JULY 13 – GOD IS WALKING WITH US

The Bible says, "Come, O house of Jacob, let us walk in the light of the LORD" (Isaiah 2:5).

Walking with us, with silent footsteps I wish I could hear more often, are my choices causing me to be deaf?

Without God I am:

Walking, happy, and content as I go down into the pit of hell.

With God I am:

Walking, and moving so He can guide and direct - (steer) my life.

Right Choices:

The neat thing about this word picture is that it gives so much excitement to life, we move in faith with Christ, knowing that He is with us. Guiding our steps and making our way right, regardless of what happens, it's ok, just walk, have faith, believe, and let Him fill this life with fullness. How awesome and amazing is this? In the end, Christ is glorified, and we are partakers of eternity with Him (see Psalm 85:13)!

July 14 – God is Purging Us

The Bible says, "Create in me a pure heart, O God, and renew a steadfast spirit within me. 11Do not cast me from your presence or take your Holy Spirit from me. 12Restore to me the joy of your salvation and grant me a willing spirit, to sustain me" (Psalms 51:10-12).

Purging us, of repented sin, and taking our desire away, and protecting us from immortal harm.

Without God I am:

Purged, of any desire to change my ways, I feed my "wants" until they haunt.

With God I am:

Purged, of a life unpleasing to God, my better choices are causing a choir of heavenly hosts to rejoice.

Right Choices:

Our greatest fulfillment in life comes when we discover our unique gifts and abilities and use them to teach others and glorify the Lord (see Isaiah 6:7).

July 15 – God is Offering Us

The Bible says, "The LORD your God is with you, he is mighty to save. He will take great delight in you, he will quiet you with his love, he will rejoice over you with singing." (Zephaniah 3:17).

Offering us, a redemptive life full of His peace, courage to do, and be free from the bondage of condemning sin.

Without God I am:

Offered, many things from the hand of Satan, this is his world for a while, but God reigns and is ready to heal my pain.

With God I am:

Offered, hope for today and freedom to not worry about tomorrow.

Right Choices:

The verb tense is never-ending, and moment to moment, daily - wow! Think of a living tree drawing nutrients from the fertile soil, sap flowing up to the leaves of our life, full of color and beauty (see Jeremiah 17:14).

July 16 – God is Filling Us

The Bible says, "Jesus replied, "If anyone loves me, he will obey my teaching. My Father will love him, and we will come to him and make our home with him" (John 14:23).

Filling us, with His goodness and desire to be like Jesus.

Without God I am:

Filled, with an appetite that eats till I bloat - I never get enough for me, and that's all she wrote.

With God I am:

Filled, with the peace that passes all understanding.

Right Choices:

Get empty of worry, strife, anxiety, fear of today, pride, hate, and lust, go up to that little icon on the computer of your brain and cut and paste it all into the recycle bin, right-click and empty it out. God, can fill it with, love, humbleness, caring, peace, trust, belief in Him, and assurance you are one of His (see Psalm 48:10).

July 17 – God is Lightening Us

The Bible says, "Grace, mercy and peace from God the Father and from Jesus Christ, the Father's Son, will be with us in truth and love" (2John 1:3).

Lightening us, of the burdens of this life and all its strife.

Without God I am:

Lightened, by the size of my portfolio, the beauty of my bride, grandeur of my home and the shine on my car.

With God I am:

Lightened, by my heart and my love for God, His people and those in need, His yoke is light.

Right Choices:

Nothing will happen to me today that God and I cannot resolve, let peace rule and be thankful for this fact (see Psalm 18:28)!

July 18 – God is Affirming Our Purpose

The Bible says, "And we know that in all things God works for the good of those who love him, who have been called according to his purpose" (Romans 8:28).

Affirming our purpose, as He weaves the pattern of life's struggles for those things He allowed to happen into a blanket of beauty.

Without God I am:

Affirming my purpose, with my drive and intent,
whatever gets in my way, I'll proudly claim my fame,
and put others to shame.

With God I am:

Affirmed, by the grace and mercy of a loving Father,
my belief and faith are growing taller.

Right Choices:

We cannot be affirmed in or by very many things in this life. The things we seem to affirm are the things that already exist as facts, but with God, it's all different and hard to imagine. His purpose for me is clear, like gravity, it will pull me to where He wants me to be, as long as I'm free to float on heaven's highway (see 1 Corinthians 15:3).

JULY 19 – GOD IS HEARKENING US

The Bible says, "The watchman opens the gate for him, and the sheep listen to his voice. He calls his own sheep by name and leads them out. 4When he has brought out all his own, he goes on ahead of them, and his sheep follow him because they know his voice" (John 10:3-5).

Calling us, in truth and spirit, to hear His word, pray and be silent with Him - do it now - hear His calling, feel His love, be strengthened.

Without God I am:

Called, to another day of indulgence in my time, doing just fine - sublime, I'm taking care of mine.

With God I am:

Called, to face the struggles within, my first Adam,
but the second Adam - Jesus abides, and as I let it go, He takes control, and I begin to grow.

Right Choices:

A calling is a special invitation to something, what's special here is that God is becoming not so special to so many. Hearken to his calling and let Him be unique to you today (see Luke 23:46)!

July 20 – God is Our Advocate

The Bible says, "My dear children, I write this to you so that you will not sin. But if anybody does sin, we have one who speaks to the Father in our defense--Jesus Christ, the Righteous One" (1John 2:1).

Our Advocate, Jesus before our Heavenly Father, pierced hands outstretched says - this one is mine and is truly divine, no sin I remember more.

Without God I am:

My advocate, in all that I act out, this is not a right place to be, I'll see - in time.

With God I am:

His advocate, one day at a time, Jesus is mine, now let me share about Thee throughout all time.

Right Choices:

An advocate makes a case for another, Christ is our advocate before the Father, and Satan is our accuser before the Father. Oh how I have humiliated Christ in front of the throne of God so many times. How can I ever give the accuser the time of day, knowing his only aim is my total damnation (see 1 John 2:1).

July 21 – God is Immanent

The Bible says, "What other nation is so great as to have their gods near them the way the LORD our God is near us whenever we pray to him" (Deuteronomy 4:7)?

Immanent, like standing near a thundering racing train,
I cannot hear nor have any fear, yet the power of this God is very near.

Without God I am:

Immanent, to the next step of unfaithful self-engrossing sin.

With God I am:

Immanent, to the realization of this living Almighty God
at work in my life.

Right Choices:

Immanent implies something as being very close. In a perfect day, you would look at me and only see Him, yes, but the journey continues, let it be so today (see John 14:17).

July 22 – God is Everywhere

The Bible Says - 24Can anyone hide in secret places so that I cannot see him?" declares the LORD. "Do not I fill heaven and earth?" declares the LORD. Jeremiah 23:24

Everywhere, with each and everyone who calls Him home,
and Lord of life, how can it be that He loves this wretched soul.

Without God I am:

Anywhere, but where I need to be, home with Jesus.

With God I am:

Somewhere, where God can use me today, part of His plan,
taking a stand - loving man.

Right Choices:

They say wherever you go, there you are, the good news is so is Christ (see Psalm 139:7-12).

July 23 – God is Setting Us Free

The Bible says, "It is for freedom that Christ has set us free. Stand firm, then, and do not let yourselves be burdened again by a yoke of slavery" (Galatians 5:1).

Setting us free, from the spiraling downward deadly effect of sin, it wants more, higher intensity and impact, until it devours us, but God breaks the chain - Jesus took the blame.

Without God I am:

Free, to dig my hole a little deeper, until this cave falls in on me.

With God I am:

Free, to choose daily Him or me, it's easier some days,
but never a done deal.

Right Choices:

What do they say about freedom? It is not free. Our freedom cost Jesus everything, which means it's not cheap. All you have to pay is just giving up self to yourself, what's that worth (see - 2 Peter 2:19)?

July 24 – God is Growing Us Slowly

The Bible says, "But the Counselor, the Holy Spirit, whom the Father will send in my name, will teach you all things and will remind you of everything I have said to you" (John 14:26).

Growing us slowly, stubborn as we are, this sin is sweet, sometimes a treat, God is patient, yet our time could be very near.

Without God I am:

Growing, like my sin, its grown deep within, I say I'll have time for God later someday, not realizing my strong sinful nature blots out desire for Him more and more.

With God I am:

Growing, slowly - in the realization of His love for me, but yet a thousand days is but a moment to God, It's ok - I'm no fraud.

Right Choices:

Growing can mean to come into being naturally what is at the root. So where are my roots planted, and from what desires am I drawing nutrients and what are they feeding (see Hebrews 8:13)?

July 25 – God is Helping Us

The Bible says, "Love must be sincere. Hate what is evil; cling to what is good" (Romans 12;9).

Helping us, <u>not</u> to love our sin, oh yes - the "hit" from gazing upon the beauty of this person - If only mine with some wine, God helps us to see them as divine - forget the wine.

Without God I am:

Helping myself to love my sin, acting out in so many ways, I feel sick, but this is one disease I don't want to lick.

With God I am:

Learning to hate my sin by considering the ultimate consequences of my sins, I see the ultimate ruin of my soul, body, heart, and mind. So I say "no", to this old show and begin to grow - slow.

Right Choices:

Helping, but more reality would be doing and changing my heart to have a new light. The point is, the source is the sauce, and it's all about the sauce (see 2 Corinthians 1:11).

JULY 26 – GOD IS CLEANING UP OUR MESS

The Bible says, "Husbands, love your wives, just as Christ loved the church and gave himself up for her 26to make her holy, cleansing her by the washing with water through the word, 27and to present her to himself as a radiant church, without stain or wrinkle or any other blemish, but holy and blameless" (Ephesians 5:25-27).

Cleaning up our mess and our broken relationship with Him - loved ones and the toll on my body and soul.

Without God I am:

Messed up, mentally and physically from the ravages of sin. I've grown accustomed to this cage and all its rage,
don't try to change this stage.

With God I am:

Cleaned up, with a new perspective and reality of what life can be - now and forever. My mind rests on His word, my eyes see His plea for me to be free.

Right Choices:

God doesn't care how bad we look or smell. He knows what the "original" me should look like. Let the restoration begin from within (see 2 Corinthians 13:9).

July 27 – God is In Control

The Bible says, "In him we were also chosen, having been predestined according to the plan of him who works out everything in conformity with the purpose of his will" (Ephesians 1:11".

In Control, it helps to know, when my anxiety is running high, wondering how I'll get by, I stop my racing mind, this God is kind and mine.

Without God I am:

In control, or so I think, I'm in free-fall toward the ground. Jesus is ready to hand me a parachute, but this "rush" is a capturing sound.

With God I am:

In control, of very little, but I am responsible for so much. My attitude, thoughts, desires, and choices, let the heavenly hosts cheer, so I hear their voices.

Right Choices:

As you watch the news on TV tonight, read the daily stories, and become so disillusioned by it all, remember this fallen world has a Savior. He is watching over you, let what He sees in you be a light in a dark world (see Isaiah 45:7).

July 28 – God is Giving Me Sight

The Bible says, "He has showed you, O man, what is good. And what does the LORD require of you? To act justly and to love mercy and to walk humbly with your God" (Micah 6:8).

Giving me sight, to see His divine purpose for everyone I meet, looking beyond the skin and eyes to seek, compassion for purpose and esteem for value of this dear soul.

Without God I am:

Building intent, getting a surface read, position my pride a bit higher, react but not feel the depth and purpose
of this soul I just met.

With God I am:

Seeing and believing that God has put each person into my life for a purpose, that each needs to be cared for, respected, and loved.

Right Choices:

Sight is the vision or perception of things. Our view is driven by our character and how the world appears by how we think - think good thoughts today, attitude – altitude (see Proverbs 3:4).

July 29 – God is An Anchor

The Bible says, "We have this hope as an anchor for the soul, firm and secure. It enters the inner sanctuary behind the curtain, 20where Jesus, who went before us, has entered on our behalf. He has become a high priest forever, in the order of Melchizedek" (Hebrew 6:19-20).

An anchor, doing what anchors do best, keeping us from going where we don't want to go, in thought, word, and deed.

Without God I am:

Anchored, to something that is going where I really don't want to go.

With God I am:

Anchored, in still waters most of the time, I pull my anchor and go just fine, He's with me across these heavy seas.

Right Choices:

An anchor provides stability and or security. We forget sometimes what we are tied to, think about the anchors in life today, and draw some conclusions about what they are doing and get rid of the bad ones (see Hebrews 6:19).

July 30 – God is To Be Feared

The Bible says, "To fear the LORD is to hate evil; I hate pride and arrogance, evil behavior and perverse speech. 14Counsel and sound judgment are mine; I have understanding and power" (Proverbs 8:13-14).

To be feared, not an easy thought for us, this reverence to behold, an awesome Almighty God, nuclear force withers before Him, imagine Him abiding within.

Without God I am:

Fearing, loss of security, loss of health and loss of love,
accept His love from above, the cross will bridge all the loss.

With God I am:

Fearing, with reverence and respect the majesty of God, He's dead serious about holiness, He hates my sin,
but He loves the sinner - amazing grace - how can it be?

Right Choices:

We often think of fear in terms of imminent danger, but with God, it's different, so we wonder. How do you fear something we don't see or comprehend? Ask Him to help with understanding here - He will (see Psalm 25:12).

July 31 – God is Cherishing Us

The Bible says, "Yet to all who received him, to those who believed in his name, he gave the right to become children of God" (John 1:12).

Cherishing us, as children of God, He made us, created us in His own likeness, each unique and special, truly for a divine purpose.

Without God I am:

Cherished, by the world for who I am, not what I am,
we chase stardom, the world is our stage, and I'm the greatest actor.

With God I am:

Cherished, as one of God's saints, by Him and those a kin,
I'm known for a tender heart, able and eager to do my part.

Right Choices:

Cherishing means to be held with dear feelings, because the "right" He gave is endowed by His dearly beloved Son. Cherish the lost today and be an instrument in cherishing others (see Ephesians 5:29).

AUGUST 1 – GOD IS WITH ME

The Bible says, "The Word became flesh and made his dwelling among us. We have seen his glory, the glory of the One and Only, who came from the Father, full of grace and truth" (John 1:14).

With me, He is holiness, wholeness, faith, health, peace, unity, joy, love, courage, strength, and life abounding.

Without God I am:

In me, I am selfish, prideful, hurtful, angry, anxious, aggressive, lusting, unloving, uncaring, and controlling.

With God I am:

With Him, I am holy and whole, faith-filled with a sense of peace, unity, and joy with His purpose, and love. Giving me courage and strength: abounding in the oneness with the Lord - healthy.

Right Choices:

Let the words that flow from my living body be a blessing today to someone. At life's end, the grave cannot speak, but the memories of what we say can last forever (see Psalm 68:18).

August 2 – God is Unseen

The Bible says, "So we fix our eyes not on what is seen, but on what is unseen. For what is seen is temporary, but what is unseen is eternal" (2Corinthians 4:18).

Unseen, but if for a moment we had such imaginative insight, such sensitivity to receive in our inner most being the impact of His courage, making us brave, fearless and divinely purposeful.

Without God I am:

Seen, as one who is contained in my own little world, careful, cunning, and careless about God.

With God I am:

Seen, as someone who is filled with compassion, a caring heart, and cleansed by the love and forgiveness of a Heavenly Father.

Right Choices:

It is hard to think about seeing something we have never seen, so how do we do this? What am I thinking that I should be seeing? Think about this; life eternal in perfect unity with the Father of life, doing things that glorify Him and bring joy to my and His heart (see 2 Corinthians 4:18).

August 3 – God is Fulfilling Us

The Bible says, "Have I not commanded you? Be strong and courageous. Do not be terrified; do not be discouraged, for the LORD your God will be with you wherever you go" (Joshua 1:9".

Fulfilling us, with hope and strength from despair and fear.
He takes our anxiety about today and enables us to think and say, "this is good" - and so we pray and go on His way.

Without God I am:

Fulfilled, with doubt and apprehension, I go on my merry way, putting whatever words out to say, the thoughts I need to win my way.

With God I am:

Fulfilled, with a sense and identity of who I am in Him, this partnership surrenders to Him, all the cares for today, guide me Lord, keep me mindful, intentional about this day.

Right Choices:

God gave manna every day in the wilderness to His children, it has to be this way - day by day, thought by thought. "Daily Redemption", be redeemed today as usual (see Revelation 2:17).

AUGUST 4 – GOD IS CONCERNED

The Bible says, "because our gospel came to you not simply with words, but also with power, with the Holy Spirit and with deep conviction. You know how we lived among you for your sake" (1Thessalonians 1:5).

Concerned, about the casualness of convictions, the lack of seriousness in intentions, and the weaknesses in in our actions. Time is running out to save the lost.

Without God I am:

Concerned, about me, respectful of others, generally - a very nice person.

With God I am:

Concerned, not as much as God would have me be for the lost.

Right Choices:

What does it take to move me? Why are my decisions so slow in coming? As the dust settles one flake at a time, and the shine is lost, take note. Let the word of life settle deep, it will sweep the dust of doubt away (see Matthew 21:21).

August 5 – God is Breaking The Chains

The Bible says, "He has showed you, O man, what is good. And what does the LORD require of you? To act justly and to love mercy and to walk humbly with your God" (Micah 6:8).

Breaking the chains, of sin deep within, our sorrow, shame, hurt, and low self-esteem, Jesus says, "come" and be washed clean - redeemed.

Without God I am:

Chained, to a pattern that is weaving a blanket of life,
wrapping me deep within, I see no sin.

With God I am:

Chained, to the purpose of the Master's plan, my decisions
begin to move from random happenings to a purpose-driven life -
that is to know the Lord and make Him known.

Right Choices:

Sin loves the sinner, and each little sin forms another "link" in the chain, so when God breaks it, what is He doing but removing its pull on me - that's a good thing, so give it up (see Acts 28:20)!

August 6 – God is The Answer

The Bible says, "yet for us there is but one God, the Father, from whom all things came and for whom we live; and there is but one Lord, Jesus Christ, through whom all things came and through whom we live" (1Corinthians 8:6).

Answer, to our striving and daily pursuit of the basic things we need. He will feed, clothe, protect, and bless us even more if we get right with Him - deep within.

Without God I am:

Answer, but a sorry one at best, I rarely seem to rest, my wealth will go to strangers, my health gives way to dangers, this love for me has grown lonely.

With God I am:

Answered, and assured by God's Holy word, seeking to know Him, I read, pray and worship, daily giving my mind, will and heart to Him.

Right Choices:

Hang it on a wall where you see it throughout the day at work, WWJD, "What Would Jesus Do?" Think about this today and every day (see John 18:3).

AUGUST 7 – GOD IS REVIVING

The Bible says, "If I had cherished sin in my heart, the Lord would not have listened; 19but God has surely listened and heard my voice in prayer. 20Praise be to God, who has not rejected my prayer or withheld his love from me (Psalms 66:18-20)!

Reviving, our sin-deadened hearts, giving us back our sensitivity and compassion - love for Him and others as we take our burdens and sin to Him.

Without God I am:

Reviving, my passion with more of what doesn't work anymore, cheap thrills, laziness, and food to celebrate this soul.

With God I am:

Revived, and quickened to the senses within, God's purpose for me today shines in my heart, with sensitivity I
pursue His desire for me today.

Right Choices:

Reviving means to put new vigor into a cause, let me be the cause of Christ today (see Ezra 9:9).

August 8 – God is Enabling Us

The Bible says, "I pray that out of his glorious riches he may strengthen you with power through his Spirit in your inner being, 17so that Christ may dwell in your hearts through faith. And I pray that you, being rooted and established in love, 18may have power, together with all the saints, to grasp how wide and long and high and deep is the love of Christ" (Ephesians 3:16-18).

Enabling us, to mediate His presence to others because our fear is great, we tremble in our struggle to share Christ. Still, Jesus says, everything is possible with God.

Without God I am:

Enabling myself to mediate my will on others, in selfish - egotistical pursuit of resentful passions.

With God I am:

Enabled by God, to have courage and strength, to live each day seeing purpose beyond my needs, Christ within me leads.

Right Choices:

While He may seem like a "silent partner", the whisper in His voice is deafening power and an enabling engine of change (see Philippians 3:21).

August 9 – God is No Insurance Policy

The Bible says, "We wait in hope for the LORD; he is our help and our shield. 21In him our hearts rejoice, for we trust in his holy name" (Psalms 33:20-21).

No insurance policy, against turmoil, strife and pain, what a cheap pious policy it would be if indeed, for the rain falls on the just and unjust, but God keeps us from all the rust.

Without God I am:

Buying insurance, and building bigger barns, they give this frail life security, I put my trust in the good I see;

With God I am:

Insured, with the presence of God in my life to guide and direct me through good and bad times, purpose not only in what I see, but what I experience inside me.

Right Choices:

We don't buy God like we may like to think at times. We buy insurance to hedge risk. We seek and love God for the reality of enlightened truth (see Psalm 19:8).

August 10 – God is Hurt

The Bible says, "And the LORD told him: "Listen to all that the people are saying to you; it is not you they have rejected, but they have rejected me as their king. 8As they have done from the day I brought them up out of Egypt until this day, forsaking me and serving other gods, so they are doing to you" (1Samuel 8:7-8).

Hurt, when we substitute prayer for contentment, have companionship with friends and things without Him,
indifference to Thee is hurting me.

Without God I am:

Hurt, by the loss of an incredible relationship that wants to be, if only I could go to bended knee, to see this Jesus, the Christ to be in me.

With God I am:

Hurt, by shallow replacements for loving not Thee, my natural human nature inclines to me, love is a choice, and so I must choose and rejoice - it is He.

Right Choices:

Hard to imagine hurting God, how can this be? We're created in His image - hurt feelings are real, think again (see Psalm 71:13).

August 11 – God is Wanting Us to Commit

The Bible says, "I know your deeds, that you are neither cold nor hot. I wish you were either one or the other! 16So, because you are lukewarm--neither hot nor cold--I am about to spit you out of my mouth" (Revelation 3:15-16).

Wanting us to commit, each day, and be aware of subtle temptations that come to mind, let the battle rage here in prayer, for heavenly hosts will roast this ghost.

Without God I am:

Wanting, to let my mind wander, fleeting thoughts squander, the real zest and purpose for this life, time is robbing me of opportunity.

With God I am:

Wanting, to be obedient to Him, I drift aimlessly in the pattern of my sin, weak chains hold tight, Jesus will give them quick flight.

Right Choices:

Sometimes I feel God is lukewarm with me, maybe even cold, distant, aloof, and not caring, and so I am with Him. But, as my energies grow weak, faith comes along, God remains and does for me what I cannot - because He cares (see Job 5:6).

August 12 – God is Not Cheap

The Bible says, "faith and knowledge resting on the hope of eternal life, which God, who does not lie, promised before the beginning of time, 3and at his appointed season he brought his word to light through the preaching entrusted to me by the command of God our Savior" Titus 1:2a

Not cheap, or a quick fix to all my ailments, I pale before this Almighty God, walking humbly in His Glory and Grace, obediently seeking His face, in all I think, do and say.

Without God I am:

Cheap, in my assessment of the value of religion, Christianity is not for me, it's but a crutch for the weak and meek.

With God I am:

Cheap, in my assessment of the value of worldly goods, my treasures are stored up in heaven and in people's lives.

Right Choices:

Cheap meaning as to have little value, it is right to so many, how do you value something you don't understand (see Romans 2:25)?

August 13 – God is Big

The Bible says, "Have I not commanded you? Be strong and courageous. Do not be terrified; do not be discouraged, for the LORD your God will be with you wherever you go" (Joshua 1:9).

Big, touching each heart, mind, and soul across the globe,
tending to the smallest detail, our minds cannot fathom,
the depth of His love for each.

Without God I am:

Big, on the little things.

With God I am:

Big, on what truly matters.

Right Choices:

When you are everywhere all the time 24/7, that's covering a lot of ground, yeah....this God is big! Don't doubt He's available to you today, right now (see Psalm 150:2)!

AUGUST 14 – GOD IS GETTING OUR ATTENTION

The Bible says, "While Ezra was praying and confessing, weeping and throwing himself down before the house of God, a large crowd of Israelites--men, women and children--gathered around him. They too wept bitterly" (Ezra 10:1).

Getting our attention, pulling our minds out of a pattern of decay, helping us to see Him and His purpose for what He wants us to be.

Without God I am:

Focused, on doing more of what I always have done, getting the same results or less, something is wrong with this mess.

With God I am:

Focused, and learning to see things right, with God's light - my thinking errors are changing, from prideful lust to trust.

Right Choices:

Don't make God cut you down to a remnant, taking it all away just so you will say - God help me. But if He does, it's ok (see Isaiah 37:31).

August 15 – God is Bringing Us Back

The Bible says, "Restore to me the joy of your salvation and grant me a willing spirit, to sustain me" (Psalms 51:12).

Bringing us back, when trust gives way to fear, and our hope seems distant and not near, the tides of life full of strife, God hears and tends to our life, we matter more to Him than anything.

Without God I am:

Going, along with a host of evil spiritual beings, if my ears could hear, my heart would be terror-stricken with fear.

With God I am:

Coming and going, and not always clear about how to steer or where to go, God whispers and takes me in tow,
beckoning me to let go of the show.

Right Choices:

Like children being led back to the promise land, hand in hand, it's sometimes painful, sometimes joyous, sometimes it's just another day of doing and being. Getting just a little bit closer to the Master's mold (see Ecclesiast 2:3).

August 16 – God is Overhauling Us

The Bible says, "but those who hope in the LORD will renew their strength. They will soar on wings like eagles; they will run and not grow weary, they will walk and not be faint" (Isaiah 40:31).

Overhauling us, from the inside out, as we open a door He shows us more, perspective heightens and burdens lighten, the fresh sweet aroma clears the mind - He's so fine!

Without God I am:

Overhauled, with cheap parts and choices that wear out way too soon, why is life so full of gloom?

With God I am:

Overhauled, from the inside out, I'm starting to figure out what life is all about, to know this Jesus - and make Him known.

Right Choices:

When we get taken apart and fixed, it may slow us down for a bit as we figure out how to get going again, these new parts of me seem strange, awkward, and needing to fit into place. Go slow for you are about to show God you're no fraud (see 2Corinthians 5:21).

August 17 – God is Serious

The Bible says, "You are not a God who takes pleasure in evil; with you the wicked cannot dwell. 5The arrogant cannot stand in your presence; you hate all who do wrong" (Psalms 5:4-5).

Serious, about the sin in our lives, He hates it!

Without God I am:

Serious, about imminent danger, if only I understood the power in a choice, led by a voice, this stranger to God is truly in danger; it's very near, if only I could hear.

With God I am:

Serious, about my need for daily time in His word, meditation, prayer, and drawing near to Him, freed from the bondage of sin.

Right Choices:

Being serious today about the casualness of a choice gone wrong puts a smile on God's face, and it will bring His grace (see 1 Peter 4:7).

August 18 – God is Our Treasure

The Bible says, (Now if you obey me fully and keep my covenant, then out of all nations you will be my treasured possession. Although the whole earth is mine" (Exodus 19:5).

Our treasure, so refined and pure, only good comes from His hand, if our heart be here, so too His blessings in our life stand.

Without God I am:

Treasured, by God in ways I don't understand, He came to save my soul, but I decided He had no role.

With God I am:

Treasured, beyond gold by God, this weary feeble life seems so shoddy, the enemy within drives this thought,
Lord lift my mind to Thine.

Right Choices:

To be treasured by God, what can it mean? Once valued, only a thief would take it away, and believe it, the thief tries every day (see Proverbs 2:1-4)!

AUGUST 19 – GOD IS WANTING FRUIT

The Bible says, "But the fruit of the Spirit is love, joy, peace, patience, kindness, goodness, faithfulness, 23gentleness and self-control. Against such things there is no law. 24Those who belong to Christ Jesus have crucified the sinful nature with its passions and desires" (Galatians 5:22-24).

Wanting fruit, in our lives, actions, and choices taken, growth in our obedience, strength in our convictions, a true sense of praise to Him.

Without God I am:

Wanting fruit, in my life to eat.

With God I am:

Fruitful, in the words I say, and I seek to bear love and kindness to others, God waters this weary soul, need I ask? - Yes! – it reminds me of who is in control.

Right Choices:

Fruit takes a season, and it is nourished at the root, every day, water your soul today in the Spirit of His love (see Colossians 1:6).

August 20 – God is Measuring Our Pain

The Bible says, "Then Jesus was led by the Spirit into the desert to be tempted by the devil. 2After fasting forty days and forty nights, he was hungry. 3The tempter came to him and said, "If you are the Son of God, tell these stones to become bread" (Matthew 4:1-3).

Measuring our pain, by the purpose in our faith, oh dear Lord how much longer must we suffer, this ordeal has numbed the zeal of this old duffer - but yes, I'm growing tougher by resting in Him.

Without God I am:

Measuring, looking for the short term payback, my patience in investing in relationships has worn thin. I can't afford to give much more, my bankrupt heart is growing dim.

With God I am:

Measuring, the contentment in my talk, the quickness in my "walk" - the cleanliness of each thought.

Right Choices:

Led by the Spirit to be tempted and after forty days He refused bread, a struggle weighs down the soul that seems so trite, let's give this a little more prayer in the fight (see 1 Corinthians 10:13)!

August 21 – God is a Flavorful Taste

The Bible says, "now that you have tasted that the Lord is good" (1Peter 2:3).

A flavorful taste, that fulfills as we hunger over a good meal, and fill our empty stomachs, so too God's love feeds our soul-nourishing life anew.

Without God I am:

Fed, with desires for "things", no lasting peace is mine.

With God I am:

Fed, with the good things of life, I seek a balance and God graciously gives what I need - not what I deserve.

Right Choices:

Chew on God today as you would prime steak and treat yourself to the dessert and sense the satisfying fulfillment of a fantastic meal. Let Him heal your soul with the flow of rich blessings - your life - truly divine (see Job 12:11).

August 22 – God is Holding Us

The Bible says, "And the peace of God, which transcends all understanding, will guard your hearts and your minds in Christ Jesus" (Philippians 4:7).

Holding us, in the grip of His hand, never letting go of this dear soul.

Without God I am:

Held, captive by influences I rarely understand, the purpose of life is clear, seek a balance for my fear, gaining pleasure with little a tear.

With God I am:

Held, captive to a gracious God that knows me deep within, He knows my every need and is ready to feed, oh to trust and let Him lead.

Right Choices:

The good news is He is holding me, that's good, because all too often I'm not holding on to Him, because I don't think I need to, but I do - hand in hand - it works better that way (see Philippians 2:16).

August 23 – God is Keeping Us

The Bible says, "The angel of the LORD encamps around those who fear him, and he delivers them" (Psalm 34:7).

Keeping us, from the negative thoughts that rampage through our minds, causing stress, illness, resentment, anger, and bitterness.

Without God I am:

Kept, in an iron cage and pattern of life, that if I could see it, the walls would go to the moon, and the foundation would go to the depths of Hell.

With God I am:

Kept, with a gracious, caring heart, full of compassion and encouragement for saint and sinner alike.

Right Choices:

Encamped around this soul, I'll share this fire with Him tonight! Can we have s'mores? I think so, yes, for sure (see Proverbs 15:3)!

August 24 – God is Healing Us

The Bible says, "But he was pierced for our transgressions, he was crushed for our iniquities; the punishment that brought us peace was upon him, and by his wounds we are healed" (Isaiah 53:5).

Healing us, and teaching us to let go of the sins of the past, asking Him to take away the remembrances, and fully feeling the freeing of any connection to old sins.

Without God I am:

Healed, by selective compartmentalization, I put stuff in a box, never to open it again, in time the pain fades, but the results shade this life I made.

With God I am:

Healed, while my sinful nature will tempt me back, on bended knee, I flee for God has enabled me to see this disease in me from which I long to be free.

Right Choices:

What does this medicine cabinet look like, bottles of love, kindness, patience, obedience, caring, forgiveness, forbearance, trust, faith, hope, and more love (see Isaiah 58:8).

August 25 – God is Victorious

The Bible says, "and, once made perfect, he became the source of eternal salvation for all who obey him 10and was designated by God to be high priest in the order of Melchizedek" (Hebrews 5:9-10).

Victorious, over Satan and all his evil powers, by the blood of Christ, reigning above all, He will raise us up too and enthrone us with Him.

Without God I am:

Victorious, in self and with the prince of this world, the forces of evil protect and deceive this soul until Sheol.

With God I am:

Victorious, in Christ, we stand one with Him, this unchanging God, whose promises of centuries past stands as true today as ever.

Right Choices:

It always feels good to be on a winning team, and this is the rose of rose bowls, the grand poobah, main event, winner take all, be good down to the finish line (see Psalm 45:4).

August 26 – God is About Submission

The Bible says, "1Submit to one another out of reverence for Christ" (Ephesians 5:21).

About submission, yes this Holy God hates sin, at its root is rebellion from authority, Lucifer wanted to be God, now we do too.

Without God I am:

Submersed, in the desires of the flesh, my pride is taking me for a ride.

With God I am:

Submersed, in a battle of wills, I do what I shouldn't, don't do what I should, Oh Lord let my striving be enabled by You thriving in my life.

Right Choices:

What does a holy God watch over, my obstinance, rebellion, casualness, the foolishness of my ways? But for a time, don't try his patience for long (see Psalm 81:15).

August 27 – God is Prospering Us

The Bible says, "The lions may grow weak and hungry, but those who seek the LORD lack no good thing" (Psalm 34:10).

Prospering us, in who we are one with Him, what we are in how we use His things, Glory to God in the highest!

Without God I am:

Prospered, in the knowledge of what things will achieve, I drink of my success to relieve the emptiness of all my gain and fame.

With God I am:

Prospered, and feeling content with the pace of the race, patience to trust, faith-giving courage, and love in my heart for all.

Right Choices:

Prospered by being one with the Lord and abiding in His grace, mercy, and love. It all goes away so quickly when I choose to depart from His path (see Daniel 4:4).

August 28 – God is A Warrior

The Bible says, "and at his appointed season he brought his word to light through the preaching entrusted to me by the command of God our Savior" (Exodus 15:3).

Warrior, His intent is clear, we better fear, this God will fight for what's right, to redeem man, now take His hand and work "The Plan."

Without God I am:

Victim, of my unyielding self, this seems so right,
forgetting my plight.

With God I am:

Warrior, this battle I daily recognize, His word has energized my purpose to be one with Him.

Right Choices:

Warriors yes, meaning we despise what the enemy is doing to this land, its people, and to me. Have no part of it, the mystery lies in letting the Lord take him on, He did it on the cross, and will do again and again (see Joel 2:11).

AUGUST 29 – GOD IS DIRECTING US

The Bible says, "It teaches us to say "no" to ungodliness and worldly passions, and to live self-controlled, upright and godly lives in this present age" (Titus 2:12).

Directing us, to incredible places, because this God is amazing, He wants only good for us - just trust - and get on His bus.

Without God I am:

Directed, by good intentions, it seems innocent enough,
but all this stuff is getting rough and tough.

With God I am:

Directed, to figure out His plan, all too confusing at times;
I keep the wheels turning and my sail in the air, so He can lead me somewhere.

Right Choices:

Directing when we let Him, it's this way because if He did it any other way, we would soon take Him for granted, thinking, well, that's just the way it is, but it's not (see Romans 6:16).

August 30 – God is Waiting To Be Known

The Bible says, "The Lord is not slow in keeping his promise, as some understand slowness. He is patient with you, not wanting anyone to perish, but everyone to come to repentance" (2Peter 3:9).

Waiting to be known, His patience runs long, for us to be strong, and praise His name and be the same on Monday as we are on Sunday.

Without God I am:

Claiming, I have no need of Him, things are quite fine within, I go my way and watch those Christians, they seem
much the same - as me.

With God I am:

Claimed, to be one of His, so what does this mean? This God who now holds, this spirit and heart so cold, come the Son like the sun to warm this soul.

Right Choices:

Repentance and redemption, two sides of a coin called faith, own it well (see 1 Chronicles 16:8).

August 31– God is Showing Us His Own

The Bible says, "There are different kinds of gifts, but the same Spirit. 5There are different kinds of service, but the same Lord. 6There are different kinds of working, but the same God works all of them in all men" (1Corinthians 12:4-6).

Showing us His own, with differences, we come together, knitting our hearts together with the love of Christ.

Without God I am:

Showing, my independence and need to be free, this freedom has chains that in the end, will reign.

With God I am:

Showing, my need to rely on Him, that every day I get by, seeking His face and all His grace, to win this race for Him.

Right Choices:

We see the mirror of Christ in our brothers and sisters, all races, the smiles on the faces radiating the love of Christ, one Spirit, one with the Lord - our Christ Jesus (see Titus 2:7).

September 1– God is Dwelling In Our Heart

The Bible says, "Now to him who is able to do immeasurably more than all we ask or imagine, according to his power that is at work within us, 21to him be glory in the church and in Christ Jesus throughout all generations, forever and ever! Amen" (Ephesians 3:20-21).

Dwelling in our heart, this God is not passive, take hold -
behold the Son, this hour may be our last, to be used of God to save the lost.

Without God I am:

Dwelling, in the security of what seems real, I like what I can touch and feel, my heart is good, better than most, all is well - but I am going to hell.

With God I am:

Dwelling, in the security of knowing, salvation is mine, so now what should I do with all this time? - Clean this heart some more - ok, but God wants me to fight this war - to win lost souls.

Right Choices:

Dwelling implies some significant space as well as a place where He likes to hang out, give Him the big chair (see Psalm 84:1).

September 2– God is Overcoming

The Bible says, "May the God of hope fill you with all joy and peace as you trust in him, so that you may overflow with hope by the power of the Holy Spirit" (Romans 15:13).

Overcoming, every storm in His time, giving peace to the mind, the battle much within, stop beating ourselves up, drink of His cup-remembering Him, and our freedom from the bondage of sin.

Without God I am:

Overcoming, the challenge from those who would strive to change my ways, by entrenching my thoughts around my beliefs, no faith I need, my faith is based on things I feel.

With God I am:

Overcoming, doubt with belief, faith with assurance, anxiety with courage, weakness with strength from above, this Jesus I love - makes it real and oh how I feel.

Right Choices:

While the world seems lost, so many problems, so little time, the soul I reach today for Him is forever grateful (see John 16:25).

September 3 – God is Creed and Conduct

The Bible says "These are the commandments the LORD proclaimed in a loud voice to your whole assembly there on the mountain from out of the fire, the cloud and the deep darkness; and he added nothing more. Then he wrote them on two stone tablets and gave them to me" (Deuteronomy 5:22).

Creed and conduct, one in step with the other, this unchanging God is cast, today and forever to the last, as the greatest Gift of all - to all.

Without God I am:

Conducting, my life in patterns of make-believe, trying to wear whatever sleeve, covers this arm and the hand it leads,
yet God sees all my ways.

With God I am:

Conducting, my life in ways I deny Christ with actions but
not with my lips. My profession unequal to practice, God restore unto me His
creed indeed.

Right Choices:

With God, they are one of the same, with a man they are not. Words talk, but my walk is like salt, it seasons a life (see Matthew 5:13).

September 4 – God is A Fisher of Men

The Bible says, "Come, follow me," Jesus said, "and I will make you fishers of men" (Matthew 4:19).

A fisher of men, women and children, so what's the bait and how does the line pull us in, this dying of self seems to chagrin: behold the Lamb feeds us peace, hope and love. God's line is strong, infinite pound test, ready to bless.

Without God I am:

Pulled, in many directions that in the end seem hopeless, to grow old and frail alone, if only I knew then what I know now - wow.....

With God I am:

Pulled, along with, stubborn as I am, this God wants to dance with me, get up - get going - times a wasting.

Right Choices:

The excitement with fishing is you never know for sure what will grab your hook and will you get it in, it's the same with evangelizing, God's got a big net, get them close to the boat, and God will do the rest, you can bet (see Mark 1:17).

September 5 – God is Using Us

The Bible says, "Dear children, let us not love with words or tongue but with actions and in truth" (1John 3:18).

Using us, and accepting our brokenness to be made whole and one with Him to be His servants, to encourage and love those in need.

Without God I am:

Used, by evil powers to hurt and confuse my heart, my choices seek urgent needs, destroying me by my deeds.

With God I am:

Used, by God in part, but He wants this whole heart, I struggle to see the purpose of the plan, yet He loves me where I stand.

Right Choices:

Yes, this is one time when it is awesome to be used, maybe even abused (see 1 Peter 1:3).

September 6 – God is Shining Upon Us

The Bible says, "May God be gracious to us and bless us and make his face shine upon us. Psalms 67:1

Shining upon us, in the stillness of the moment. His radiance is mine. This awesome God fills us up, with faith, hope, and courage to love, showing us His way, stronger each day.

Without God I am:

Shining, on the outside more then on the inside, the rays
reflect my ways, you can see where I've been, this trail
is littered with all my sin.

With God I am:

Shining, with the blessed assurance that Jesus is mine, God
almighty indwelling for all time, I take it so lightly, yet He holds
me so tightly.

Right Choices:

The closer you get, the brighter He gets (se Exodus 34:29).

September 7 – God is A Better Way

The Bible says, "What is more, I consider everything a loss compared to the surpassing greatness of knowing Christ Jesus my Lord, for whose sake I have lost all things. I consider them rubbish, that I may gain Christ" (Philippians 3:8).

A better way, many would say, but we fail to pursue Him because we love our sin, yet what gain it brings, a moment of pleasure for an eternity of lost treasure.

Without God I am:

Better, because you get yours and I got mine, we're just fine for all time.

With God I am:

Better, His goodness abides deep within my heart, helping me to do my part with a loving heart.

Right Choices:

So, why doesn't it seem better to so many? You would think if it was true, this would all be a done deal, but it's not, why not? The God so many chose to follow is I. It all starts and ends with me, as it will in eternity in hell (see Psalm 31:19).

September 8 – God is Taking

The Bible says, "and if you call out for insight and cry aloud for understanding, 4and if you look for it as for silver and search for it as for hidden treasure, 5then you will understand the fear of the LORD and find the knowledge of God" (Proverbs 2:3-5).

Taking, me and mine and giving in its place Thee and Thine, replacing my terror and despair with the assurance of forgiveness from this repentant heart.

Without God I am:

Taking, me and mine for granted, bored so often with what's been planted, I pick the fruit, but I just don't give a hoot.

With God I am:

Giving, where there is hatred - love, despair - hope, darkness - light, sadness - joy; to other saints and sinners alike in my life.

Right Choices:

Be careful what you take today, we take too much, give too little and hang onto the things that don't matter. Let God have it, you'll like the way you look (see 2 Thessalonians 1:8).

September 9 – God is Forgetting

The Bible says, "Remember not the sins of my youth and my rebellious ways; according to your love remember me, for you are good, O LORD" (Psalm 25:7).

Forgetting, our past and error-filled ways, building in us the character that does not sway, our value is rich in who we are in Him - not what we are at the gym.

Without God I am:

Forgetting, about my why, I pursue my what. My who don't care about how. When is now, and my where passes me by with a stare.

With God I am:

Forgetting, that God is good and He lets past sin go, I drag it back to the throne of grace and taunt myself. But, God says surrender to his cleansing grace within and be renewed.

Right Choices:

So, why can't I, why do I keep dragging it up to God, a friend, my mate, my family - let it go! Whatever it is, God is bigger, be smaller, let Him have it. Stand firm today in God's goodness and grace, it belongs to you in Him (see Deuteronomy 4:23)!

September 10 – God is Granting

The Bible says, "Restore to me the joy of your salvation and grant me a willing spirit, to sustain me" (Psalm 51:12).

Granting, all that we have is from Him, the choice alone for us is how shall we receive what has been given - with thanksgiving!

Without God I am:

Receiving, from the hands of my efforts, believing God's hand was abandoned from this effort.

With God I am:

Receiving, the good and the bad, knowing that God has allowed and granted this to me, weaving a pattern to set me free - thankful.

Right Choices:

We seem more ready for enlightenment than we realize, it's a precious gift, not cheap, not to be trampled. We change slowly and trust too lightly and see too dimly. He gives as best we can endure daily with a little bit of "new", but with tons of grace and mercy, ever pouring into our lives (see Proverbs 8:21).

September 11 – God is Thinking

The Bible says, "if my people, who are called by my name, will humble themselves and pray and seek my face and turn from their wicked ways, then will I hear from heaven and will forgive their sin and will heal their land" (2Chronicles 7:14).

Thinking, about the depth of our heart, looking deep into our soul, He knows all, lovingly He guides us to a better place.

Without God I am:

Thinking, about this day, and or the next, my mind fixed on how to move, what to say. God get out of my way.

With God I am:

Thinking, anxiously about my future, my mind races to places I would rather not go, but God assures me He has a plan, I must trust Him and let Him guide this fan.

Right Choices:

We would be better served by thinking more about what we think God is thinking and less about what I think others are thinking (see Psalm 64:5).

September 12 – God is Honest

The Bible says, "All a man's ways seem right to him, but the LORD weighs the heart" (Proverbs 21:2).

Honest, about everything - He has no reason to conceal, for His actions, motives, and heart are pure - He gives the same to us for sure.

Without God I am:

Honest, about some things, I paint the picture well, it looks good on the outside, but to walk the halls of this mind, you will find - pictures of pride, plans of self-will, and chains of lustful passions.

With God I am:

Honest, about some things, I hope for my faith to keep pace with the race. I want to be fine, but I'm anxious in time, Hold me Jesus - I'm shaking like a leaf.

Right Choices:

Why is honesty so important, and why does God treasure it so much? Because in the end, it's all about "truth" and the "promise" and the hope we have in Christ and what He did and what He has said and who He really is – God (see Proverbs 12:17).

September 13 – God is Condemning

The Bible says, "Whoever believes in him is not condemned, but whoever does not believe stands condemned already because he has not believed in the name of God's one and only Son" (John 3:18).

Condemning, all sin not covered by the blood of Jesus Christ, to Hell for all eternity.

Without God I am:

Condemned, by my choice to ignore the reality of Christ, His saving grace and desire to dwell within my heart, I choose to lose eternity in heaven for eternity in hell.

With God I am:

Condemned, when I fail to forgive myself and others, God harbors no grudge against me when I seek His forgiveness, He expects me to do the same.

Right Choices:

This is a fearful and strong word that echoes through the canyons of sin and corruption that so prevails in this world. As we read Isaiah, the seriousness of our wayward ways stands condemned and destroyed in time (see Isaiah 3:13).

September 14 – God is Responsible

The Bible says, "Then I saw a great white throne and him who was seated on it. Earth and sky fled from his presence, and there was no place for them. 12And I saw the dead, great and small, standing before the throne, and books were opened. Another book was opened, which is the book of life. The dead were judged according to what they had done as recorded in the books" (Revelation 20:11-12).

Responsible, to live up to His word, which is inerrant – perfect and all revealing about His character and what He expects of us.

Without God I am:

Responsible, for living my life and face the consequences of the Great White Throne Judgement!

With God I am:

Responsible, for what God has revealed to me, I'll be held to a higher standard, He expects me not to ignore Him.

Right Choices:

I am called today to make a response and be full of action in a way that is proactive and purposeful around my values (see Luke 12:48).

September 15 – God is Showing Us

The Bible says, "But God demonstrates his own love for us in this: While we were still sinners, Christ died for us. 9Since we have now been justified by his blood, how much more shall we be saved from God's wrath through him" (Romans 5:8-9)!

Showing us, how to live our life in submission to Him. These words are so easy to write, so difficult to do, it's not in our striving, but in our thriving to release our heart to Him.

Without God I am:

Showing myself, how it works best when I can control the plan, I drive hard to be the man.

With God I am:

Showing Jesus, how much I love Him by my obedience to Him in full surrender.

Right Choices:

Showing God how much I love him by what I do in His power (see Romans 12:10).

September 16 – God is Making Our Life

The Bible says, "For we are to God the aroma of Christ among those who are being saved and those who are perishing" (2Corinthians 2:15).

Making our life, a better place, full of grace, compassion, abiding confidence, and strength with obedient focus. Our going is coming around to show us a better place.

Without God I am:

Making my life, a roadway littered with indulgence, greed,
fear, anxiety, hatred, pride, selfishness, lust, and the
stench of all my sin.

With God I am:

Making my life, a roadway flowered with a sweet, wholesome fragrance of Him.

Right Choices:

The good news here is that God does not do it all at once, it's moment to moment, daily redemption. Keep moving, some days faster than others, but keep moving (see Psalm 40:2).

September 17 – God is Living In Us

The Bible says, "And I will ask the Father, and he will give you another Counselor to be with you forever –17 the Spirit of truth. The world cannot accept him, because it neither sees him nor knows him. But you know him, for he lives with you and will be in you" (John 14:16-17).

Living in us, we are lost without Him, desperate for Him,
His broken self given within.

Without God I am:

Living, taking the good with the bad, when I'm sad, I'll grab the next fad.

With God I am:

Living, as though the end times may never come, but then I stop and think, this stinks, in a blink it could all sink, better now behold His fold and grow bold.

Right Choices:

We don't see what we don't know, reading the puzzle with missing pieces, the word with missing letters, a sunset without the sun, we see because we know because He tells us (see 1 Timothy 4:10).

September 18 – God is Love of Our Life

The Bible says, "This is love: not that we loved God, but that he loved us and sent his Son as an atoning sacrifice for our sins" (1John 4:10).

Love of our life, with His arms around, we seek to be strong, hearing His song, Lord let our life abound.

Without God I am:

Loving, possession of passion, as I grow old, my wrinkles and flab begin to blab, I'm not as beautiful as some, but wit
will cover it, keep it dim-lit.

With God I am:

Loving, more from the inside, I'm becoming more beautiful
every day, this heart shines with holiness - pure and clean,
quality that is now redeemed.

Right Choices:

What makes this word so powerful is the source of all love, the living Christ, and His living word. Let this word abound in your life today (see 1 Peter 1:3).

September 19 – God is Liberty

The Bible says, "What shall we say, then? Shall we go on sinning so that grace may increase? 2By no means! We died to sin; how can we live in it any longer" (Romans 6:1-2)?

Liberty, is freeing us from the slavery of our sin deep within.

Without God I am:

Enslaved, to my thought patterns of life, my perspective adds to my strife, God wants me to see anew, how His caring - compassionate love is there for me too.

With God I am:

Free, to see God in a new light, my new sight is right, I let go and let my mind flow to the power of this Jesus to control.

Right Choices:

I get this funny thought on rare occasions, I need to ask my parents if this is OK, but they have long passed from this life. I smile and think, I'm free to choose. When we are one with the Lord, it's like riding a bike on a good day, just remember the basics, and you will do OK (see - Luke 4:18).

September 20 – God is Displacing Our Self

The Bible says, "In the same way, count yourselves dead to sin but alive to God in Christ Jesus. 12Therefore do not let sin reign in your mortal body so that you obey its evil desires" (Romans 6:11-12).

Displacing our self, with Thee - our religion is so often about us, our harmony with God, our peace of mind, our health. God help us to abandon self like a sinking ship and simply seek You.

Without God I am:

Self ruled, and focused for now on me, just like hell will be, nothing but eternal life totally focused on self and my torment.

With God I am:

Self reliant, way too much, forgive me Lord for my life feels so fragile, I want to be more agile, caring for others and sharing my time, an e-mail, phone call, a smile, or a good story with a friend.

Right Choices:

Displacing what is my natural-born sinful self with a willingness to be changed and made new. My willingness a gift as well, from obedience, won from the Son (see Romans 6:13).

SEPTEMBER 21 – GOD IS AN OASIS

The Bible says, "Above all else, guard your heart, for it is the wellspring of life" (Proverbs 4:23).

An oasis, for out of the sands the wellspring of life,
He makes something good of us, feeding us living water
to nourish us.

Without God I am:

A spiritual desert, barren and dry - a landscape of boulders
without eternal purpose, the dark side of this life a scary place to go.

With God I am:

A spiritual garden, needing to be weeded, for with the flowers were
seeded, weeds that bleed the life from creed,
may all that grows be beautiful.

Right Choices:

An oasis is a place or thing offering welcome relief as from difficulty, so it is with the Lord, stand freely in the shade of grace (see -Zechariah 9:1).

September 22 – God is a Thought Away

The Bible says, "How precious to me are your thoughts, O God! How vast is the sum of them" (Psalm 139:17).

Thought away, or nearer so, our heart beats with the oneness of His spirit, free but let us not be deceived.

Without God I am:

Thinking, that life is what it is and what it has become, there is simply no more to it.

With God I am:

Thinking, too often that my freedom has released me from everything - including God. My prayer convicts me through His spirit of my reliance on self.

Right Choices:

Cultivate gladness and thankfulness with every breath of thought, it nourishes the soul (see 1 Corinthians 13:11).

September 23 – God is Gladness

The Bible says, "In him our hearts rejoice, for we trust in his holy name. 22May your unfailing love rest upon us, O LORD, even as we put our hope in you" (Psalms 33:21-22).

Gladness, because the essence of who we have become rings clear to God's ear, He's happy we are near.

Without God I am:

Glad, when I show kindness to others and they return appreciation, but a thankless reaction brings madness.

With God I am:

Glad, when I put aside the toils of the day, take time to read His word and pray, meditate on these "panels" and see the true character of God and His desire for me.

Right Choices:

Joy is the wonder of God as lived today, pray, and say, thank you, Jesus, for being one with me today (see Psalm 45:7).

September 24 – God is Inescapable

The Bible says, "No temptation has seized you except what is common to man. And God is faithful; he will not let you be tempted beyond what you can bear. But when you are tempted, he will also provide a way out so that you can stand up under it" (1Corinthians 10:13).

Inescapable, He is a friend by our side at every moment of every day - talk to Him, tell Him honestly how you feel, He'll minister as we kneel.

Without God I am:

Escaping, to things that attempt to fill a giant void, I run from God, believing I can't give up my ways: besides, they are not so bad.

With God I am:

Escaping, the toils of countless sins uncommitted because the Lord has weaved into this heart, a new desire for Him.

Right Choices:

Inescapable in that God will see me around it, or deal with my transgression if I pass through it; either way, He is there. While passing through, it may seem sweet, but in the end, it's no treat (see Proverbs 19:5).

September 25 – God is Bringing Us Through

The Bible says, "I am the living bread that came down from heaven. If anyone eats of this bread, he will live forever. This bread is my flesh, which I will give for the life of the world" (John 6:51).

Bringing us through, each day as it becomes the present, then the future, my anxiety is gone - almost - just hold on.

Without God I am:

Passing through, this town called life, maybe I'll build a store here, buy some ice, check out the restaurant, or just speed on through.

With God I am:

Passing through, this town called life, maybe I'll stop and talk, see a friend in need, bring a meal to feed, encourage a hungry soul.

Right Choices:

The menu is living bread from heaven, and the promise is immortality. We've been looking for it all our lives, but never realized we have found it. This is deep water (see 2 Timothy 1:10).

September 26 – God is Burying His Workmen

The Bible says, "Jesus said to him, "Let the dead bury their own dead, but you go and proclaim the kingdom of God" (Luke 9:60).

Burying His workmen, but He carries on the work with saint and sinner alike, we come but for a short time, but this time changes destiny for all time for many.

Without God I am:

Buried, naked going out as I came in, with all my sin.

With God I am:

Buried, naked going out as I came in, with all my sin
given over to Him.

Right Choices:

It's a scary thought not to matter to Jesus. Like chaff in the wind, a life lived and lost, gone, off the map, no one cares anymore, no one, hope gone, lost, wasted, alone with misery and contempt for eternity. This is as bad as it gets. What would this really be like? Yes, let the dead bury their own, they're all lost, so proclaim life while breath and blood flow, it's the only row to hoe (see Psalm 31:12).

September 27 – God is Our Joy Alone

The Bible says, "I will be glad and rejoice in your love, for you saw my affliction and knew the anguish of my soul" (Psalm 31:7).

Our joy alone, so let our rejoicing be solely focused on the fact, that we are children of God - chosen by Him

Without God I am:

Chosen, to be left alone except by the saving grace of Christ, who desires that none be lost.

With God I am:

Chosen, to open my heart, mind, and soul to Him, letting Him in to free me from sin, the bondage that keeps my decisions cheap.

Right Choices:

The joy of the Lord escapes me all too often, you need to help me here, Lord. The circumstances that weigh on my life over shadow joy. Values are messed up and out of proportion, I just don't get it, so help me here. Let me be a willing bondservant today (see 1 Chronicles 16:23).

September 28 – God is Depending On Us

The Bible says, "Don't let anyone look down on you because you are young, but set an example for the believers in speech, in life, in love, in faith and in purity. 13Until I come, devote yourself to the public reading of Scripture, to preaching and to teaching (1Timothy 4:12-13).

Depending on us, because He's our friend. The badge of a friend is to help do whatever needs to be done…. there are many needs.

Without God I am:

Dependent, on myself and the friendships I have in common with selected people, my tolerance is low for the no-show when I needed help.

With God I am:

Dependent, on my Heavenly Father for my every need. The courage to go on, the strength to be His person, serving His every need - to feed the flock.

Right Choices:

Depending on us to rely on Him, to let Him in, to be the source of our strength. So, what's pulling on you to sin, pride, anxiety, fear, lust, indulgence, or just a way to casual self-sufficiency, don't go it alone (see Job 39:11).

September 29 – God is Magnified

The Bible says, "Be exalted, O LORD, in your strength; we will sing and praise your might" (Psalm 21:13).

Magnified, so that others might see, this awesome amazing God, magnified in our lives as living sacrifices for Thee.

Without God I am:

Magnified, with a burning desire to be seen, heard and subject to the ways of my means.

With God I am:

Magnifying, a Holy God with the obedience of my will.

Right Choices:

God is magnified and glorified when we give it all to Him. The honor and recognition are all deserving for the blessings that have been granted (see 1 Chronicles 17:24).

SEPTEMBER 30 – GOD IS AUTHOR OF OUR FAITH

The Bible says, "I want you to know, brothers, that the gospel I preached is not something that man made up. 12I did not receive it from any man, nor was I taught it; rather, I received it by revelation from Jesus Christ" (Galatians 1:11).

Author of our faith, and perfector of our lives and will, we grow when we don't even know, He's changing our pathway, keeping Satan at bay everyday.

Without God I am:

The author, along with legions of evil spirits, making my life seem right, spiritually blinded by pride, this ride has lied but seemed so tied to so many good things.

With God I am:

Authored, by the hand of God daily, I seek His Spirit in prayer, mindful throughout the day, to stay sensitive to the temptations in my mind that lead me astray.

Right Choices:

This life book is still being written, many lives don't end so well. The biblical narrative is full of them. God writes the manual for how to make it right, life is not always intuitive, read the manual and put it together right - the first time (see 2 Timothy 1:11).

October 1– God is Believing In Us

The Bible says, "if my people, who are called by my name, will humble themselves and pray and seek my face and turn from their wicked ways, then will I hear from heaven and will forgive their sin and will heal their land" (2Chronicles 7:14)

Believing in us, not in part but in a wholesomeness
that says we are good in His sight, blameless and forgiven,
shameless, and free to be all that He has planned for me.

Without God I am:

Believing in me, I have high standards, I'm fair-minded,
kind, loving, and encouraging to others - it all seems so spiritual.

With God I am:

Believing, in part, that this God is who He says He is, but my mind can't go to see the whole show. However, glimpses of Him leave me awestruck and amazed as He takes me in tow.

Right Choices:

"If" is such a small word here with such a huge meaning and impact, so big, so big ..... Let "if" reign today (see Matthew 21:22)!

October 2– God is Wellspring of Life

The Bible says, "Above all else, guard your heart, for it is the wellspring of life" (Proverbs 4:23).

Wellspring of life, in our darkness, we learn to need light, in our times of unhappiness and pain we learn more of Him as we draw near to His breast and take rest.

Without God I am:

Springing, to eternal death with happiness and friends, I buzz from flower to flower. This hour I feel my power.

With God I am:

Springing, to eternal life from my unhappiness, resentments, moods of black despair, accepting what cannot be changed, I yield my will to let Him fill, me with faith - hope and love.

Right Choices:

A good heart needs to be guarded by trustful friends, a loving mate and believing that God loves me as much as He ever will (see Psalm 9:10).

October 3 – God is Grace

The Bible says, "God opposes the proud but gives grace to the humble." 6Humble yourselves, therefore, under God's mighty hand, that he may lift you up in due time. 7Cast all your anxiety on him because he cares for you"(1Peter 5:5-7).

Grace, pardoning us from all our sins, God one with the Son, we are accepted and loved by Jesus Christ, we are a flower with His power in His sight.

Without God I am:

Robed, with Satan, he claims this soul, which he
stole with lies, deception, and passions out of control.

With God I am:

Robed, with Christ, who gave me a new life, my eyes are tempted, my mind flirts with sin - sometimes giving in, knowing it's wrong, the victory is to the one in whom I'm strong.

Right Choices:

Grace is the unmerited love and favor of God towards me, when I need it most, I'm most likely to get it the least, because when I'm doing the things that beg for grace, I'm not in a good place. The place I need to be is Humbleville (see Romans 5:2).

October 4 – God is Empowering Us

The Bible says, "For in my inner being I delight in God's law; 23but I see another law at work in the members of my body, waging war against the law of my mind and making me a prisoner of the law of sin at work within my members. 24What a wretched man I am! Who will rescue me from this body of death (Romans 7:22-24)?

Empowering us, to wage battle with temptation before it becomes sin and willful disobedience, by simply asking us to call on His name, Lord - help me.

Without God I am:

Empowered, by forces unseen and unheard, deep within - so God sent His Son, He gave us His Word and gave us the Holy Spirit, so that the race could be won.

With God I am:

Empowered, with His love that runs deep, the power is in the shower of His blood, that covered all my sin, remember now who I am in Him, when temptation knocks on the door of sin.

Right Choices:

Sin, I hear you knocking but you can't come in (see 1 Corinthians 12:11).

October 5 – God is Quieting Us

The Bible says, "To the roots of the mountains I sank down; the earth beneath barred me in forever. But you brought my life up from the pit, O LORD my God" (Jonah 2:6).

Quieting us, as pain from disease and age whips our minds, as fear of worldly worries ties knots all about, a gracious God calms our spirit - giving strength and courage, medicating our soul with His love

Without God I am:

Quieted, by the addictive drug of a challenge, food, alcohol, and sex, I feed my body what it needs to succeed and believe.

With God I am:

Quieted, in the calm after the storm, this tornado experience just devastated my norm. I can't believe what I see, but God rushes in to relieve my fear within, His powerful might makes the storm so slight.

Right Choices:

How low can I go? It will never be below the arms of Jesus. The quiet He brings dispelled my fear, soothed my sorrow, wrapped anxiety up in His plan for my life, a sacrifice (see Psalm 131:2).

OCTOBER 6 – GOD IS SECURITY

The Bible says, "Therefore my heart is glad and my tongue rejoices; my body also will rest secure, 10because you will not abandon me to the grave, nor will you let your Holy One see decay" (Psalms 16:9-10).

Security, what is it deep within that cries for safety, comfort, and normalcy? A fragile strength, that when God draws near – His awesome force strengthens us like a horse.

Without God I am:

Secure, in what I wonder, health can vanish, friends go away, money goes as I play, beauty ages, jobs are gone in stages, the angel of death is knocking, now what? - "I'm toast".

With God I am:

Secure, but not feeling it as much as I should, or could if I would just take some time, not a lot but some, to stop and rest on the thought - Jesus is mine!

Right Choices:

When we get to a point where we can give up our life and take His, the mystery of faith found, few find it, but those that do truly live (see Job 24:23).

OCTOBER 7 – GOD IS HOLDING US ACCOUNTABLE

The Bible says, "But I tell you that men will have to give account on the day of judgment for every careless word they have spoken. 37For by your words you will be acquitted, and by your words you will be condemned." (Matthew 12:36-37).

Holding us accountable, He blesses those He can trust. He gives a little before He gives us a lot, don't let it rot, use what you got - it's a lot.

Without God I am:

Accountable, for the total impact of my life and the effect it has on others, not only my loss but how I caused others to lose as well - now in hell - and those on their way.

With God I am:

Accountable, to God for every thought, word, and deed, my only hope at the end of my rope, is that He sees Himself in me, covered and free.

Right Choices:

One day we will all give an account of our lives, what we have done with what He gave, the gifts of the spirit that made each truly unique. Don't get this wrong, it's not about being strong, but being weak and reliant on His loving care (see Romans 3:19).

October 8 – God is Not Tempting Us

The Bible says, "For we do not have a high priest who is unable to sympathize with our weaknesses, but we have one who has been tempted in every way, just as we are--yet was without sin. 16Let us then approach the throne of grace with confidence, so that we may receive mercy and find grace to help us in our time of need" (Hebrews 4:15-18).

Not tempting us, but He is testing us, will we run to our sin when the lights get dim, or will we learn to trust in Him?

Without God I am:

Tempted, so that this sin doesn't seem like sin anymore. I've normalized my behavior, in spite of the Savior.

With God I am:

Tempted, on the surface, it looks and feels so good - just as it should, but a thoughtful mind in-dwelt with the sublime takes the integral of sin to the extreme to expose the horrific scheme.

Right Choices:

Tempted to think that I can lick this thing, not return to my vomit, but it's not true, I can't. The mystery here lies in wanting Jesus more than my sin, and He knows it. So, what's it going to be, me or Him (see 1 Timothy 6:9)?

October 9 – God is Focused

The Bible says, "Trust in the LORD forever, for the LORD, the LORD, is the Rock eternal" (Isaiah 26:4).

Focused, because His purpose and priorities are clear, through complex issues He can steer, one step at a time, the process is becoming mine.

Without God I am:

Distracted, this moment with the thought process of how I will accomplish things, It seems right, but there are many fights, I'll work to make it happen with all my might.

With God I am:

Focusing, on the goal, I make my vision and purpose clear, Jesus is near to steer my every thought that is dear, my peers sense the mission, and the dream is caught, we're on our way, I'm happy to say.

Right Choices:

A focused life has a proactive purpose and mission written all over it. Are you drifting along, wondering why something is the way it is? Not a hair falls from our head without God knowing it (see Philippians 3:12-14).

October 10 – God is Promising

The Bible says, "Keep your lives free from the love of money and be content with what you have, because God has said, "Never will I leave you; never will I forsake you." 6So we say with confidence, " The Lord is my helper; I will not be afraid. What can man do to me" (Hebrew 13:5-6)?

Promising, a new covenant with us: laws not written on tablets, but rather written on our hearts and minds. Our forgiven wickedness remembered no more - thus declares the Lord.

Without God I am:

Promised, what and where can I read any word, if I want to follow Satan, where is his book of promises, what does it say, how will he help me, what is the eternal picture? The Bible has answers!

With God I am:

Promised, that He will never leave me nor forsake me, oh Jesus come near me now, wipe my brow of this worry, let me take hold of His strength and peace as I hurry.

Right Choices:

Promises with man are made to be broken, with God there is no joking (see Joshua 21:45)!

October 11 – God is A Repairman

The Bible says, "He said, "If you listen carefully to the voice of the Lord your God and do what is right in his eyes, if you pay attention to his commands and keep all his decrees, I will not bring on you any of the diseases I brought on the Egyptians, for I am the Lord, who heals you" (Exodus 15:26).

Repairman, our bones break, and He heals them, we choose to sin, and He hears our prayers and forgives us, we recognize our helplessness. He renews a right spirit within us.

Without God I am:

A demolition man, I know how to take things apart better then I know how to put them together. I'm good at breaking relationships, casting fear into others, putting others down.

With God I am:

A walking miracle, God took a lost, broken and messed up person and set my feet on firm ground, to be led by His Spirit, contrite - redeemed and whole - now found.

Right Choices:

With a willing heart, the pain is gone quickly, and what is left in place of brokenness and illness is wholeness and wellness (see Psalm 51:10).

October 12 – God is A Divine Companion

The Bible says, "Praise be to the God and Father of our Lord Jesus Christ, the Father of compassion and the God of all comfort, 4who comforts us in all our troubles, so that we can comfort those in any trouble with the comfort we ourselves have received from God" (2Corinthians 1:3-4).

A divine companion is like the wind that comes and fills slack sails, the fragrance that arises from a rose, so our God comes to lift our spirits from our woes.

Without God I am:

A companion, to many but friend to few, I give and give and seem to get so little in return, I am starting to burn, not sure where to turn.

With God I am:

A companion, to the Lord of hosts, I've taken advantage of this friendship way too many times, but this God keeps coming back, wishing I had never left.

Right Choices:

Imagine a friend so close, but I feel so alone, but yet in an instant, He is there, within, giving care. The presence is so real, yet surreal, a divine mystery - trust and obey: this is faith at its best (see Psalm 119:63).

October 13 – God is Linking Us

The Bible says, "Are not all angels ministering spirits sent to serve those who will inherit salvation" (Hebrews 1:14)?

Linking us, to a company of angels, unseen friends on the other side, risen souls on a higher plane, are all involved in how we play our lowly way.

Without God I am:

Linked, to thought patterns that come from who knows where, I dress my emotions with care. I want them to look good, if only I could - feel as good.

With God I am:

Linked, to a loving God who keeps track of the smallest details of my life, He knows my strife, my purpose is becoming clear, I'm keeping my fear near His ear.

Right Choices:

Ministering spirits from the almighty powerful throne of God, the great I Am, don't doubt this clout which is about to wage the battle you need not fight (see Matthew 4:11).

October 14 – God is Thanking Us

The Bible says, "in order that in the coming ages he might show the incomparable riches of his grace, expressed in his kindness to us in Christ Jesus" (Ephesians 2:7).

Thanking us, for every good deed done to another, for it is as though we did it for Him and to Him.

Without God I am:

Thankful, for the good things other people do for me.

With God I am:

Thankful, that my life has balance, it also has perspective, I know my God Lord Jesus, and He knows me.

Right Choices:

One of the most challenging things we do is being thankful to God. It seems trite that God would thank us, but we are made in His image and as it is our nature as we grow in Him to be so thankful for the kind things people do for us each day, so it is with Him. Remember today as the neat things occur that make you smile, just say, thank you, Jesus (see Colossians 3:16).

October 15 – God is Mending Lives

The Bible says, "A bruised reed he will not break, and a smoldering wick he will not snuff out, till he leads justice to victory" (Matthew 12:20).

Mending lives, He takes our broken relationship with Him and restores it. Calling us back to fellowship in prayer, our brokenness caused by unrepentant sin, thank you, Jesus, nice to be with you again.

Without God I am:

Mending things, that wear out, and ultimately I throw it out. Nothing lasts forever, all things have a time and place, just like me, then gone forever - my eternal purpose exists – for whatever.

With God I am:

Mending things, in people's lives, because we are in this together, we help make it better, loving saint and sinner as we go.

Right Choices:

Mending is something mothers in days gone by would do endlessly because buying new was not possible. We have this one life, precious as it is and worn, it needs mending (see Lamentations 5:21).

October 16 – God is A Depository

The Bible says, "And you also were included in Christ when you heard the word of truth, the gospel of your salvation. Having believed, you were marked in him with a seal, the promised Holy Spirit, 14who is a deposit guaranteeing our inheritance until the redemption of those who are God's possession--to the praise of his glory" (Ephesians 1:13-14).

A depository, where sin and shame are locked away and forgotten, it's a room full of Satan's lies, so horrific, and we thank God for the lies we never lived out.

Without God I am:

Deposited, with the belief that I'm ok - I've got my rough spots, but who doesn't, don't try to make me feel guilty, this religion stuff is a bunch of fluff.

With God I am:

Deposited, with the experience of a real God, He redeems my heart, mind, and soul, as I surrender my stubborn will and ask Him to daily guide me home.

Right Choices:

Positioned with the seal of eternity, yet living in a natural sinful body, each moment and day given to serve, but whom (see 2 Timothy 1:14).

OCTOBER 17 – GOD IS MAKING US

The Bible says, "But rejoice that you participate in the sufferings of Christ, so that you may be overjoyed when his glory is revealed" (1Peter 4:13).

Making us, brave and courageous as we face hardship, sorrow, and fear of circumstances. Blessed by all our failure of results, for in our failure - God builds character and fearless leadership.

Without God I am:

Made, weak, and stubborn by the challenge of trials, I live in denial, that my sins have piled, a heavy load to carry down this road of life.

With God I am:

Made, of great hope as God works within, helping me not to sin, as I surrender to Him, I walk into the face of fear, knowing He is near - filling me with strength very dear.

Right Choices:

This is deep water, suffering in the cross of Christ, how do we understand what this means? Cultivate gladness for redemption lives by His Holy Spirit in a mortal body with an eternal soul, freed from the bondage of the body; enjoy this precious privilege, the gift of Christ (see Psalm 130:1).

October 18 – God is Grounding

The Bible says, "the sinful mind is hostile to God. It does not submit to God's law, nor can it do so. 8Those controlled by the sinful nature cannot please God. 9You, however, are controlled not by the sinful nature but by the Spirit, if the Spirit of God lives in you. And if anyone does not have the Spirit of Christ, he does not belong to Christ" (Romans 8:7-9).

Grounding, our sin and neutralizing its force, because we choose to divorce, and let go of the foe, that was taking its toll - as it stole my peace and joy.

Without God I am:

Grounded, with both feet in a sinking stinking hole, I sink deeper, not knowing the reaper is about to snatch this keeper.

With God I am:

Grounded, in the reality of Christ, my life has a new meaning, my life is bigger than my circumstance, this God has a plan, and He wants me to dance, enjoying the journey before me.

Right Choices:

The attacks are new each day. Thoughts that push deep into passions and weaknesses that exist deep within, like static energy, seeking a path, strap onto Jesus fast (see Psalm 39:1).

October 19 – God is Soothing

The Bible says, "My son, pay attention to what I say; listen closely to my words. 21Do not let them out of your sight, keep them within your heart; 22for they are life to those who find them and health to a man's whole body" (Proverbs 4:20-22).

Soothing, our pain, quieting our soul, calming our spirit, bringing peace to our mind and joy to our heart, meditatee on this. His presence will be bliss, yes, Lord.

Without God I am:

Soothed, when I receive a kind word from a friend, achieve a successful conquest, a full stomach, quieted demands from others, and the forgotten pain of my sin.

With God I am:

Soothed, by yielding to His awesome amazing power, I let Him take control of my situation, His love is great - and so will be my fate.

Right Choices:

Be soothed by the goodness of God, for with it comes a lasting food that enriches the soul (see Isaiah 18:4).

OCTOBER 20 – GOD IS IN OUR EVERY EXPERIENCE

The Bible says, "While he was still speaking, a bright cloud enveloped them, and a voice from the cloud said, "This is my Son, whom I love; with him I am well pleased. Listen to him" (Matthew 17:5)!

In our every experience, the challenge for us is to let Him make a difference in the outcome, or will we continue to run from this loving Son.

Without God I am:

Running, somewhere where past roads have taken many, the places have familiar faces, worldly security, my friends, job, health, and the things that count for winning races.

With God I am:

Trying to see, God in me, sometimes it flees - because I'm too focused on me, this battle of wills is a fight to be had, that Jesus the Son has already won - be glad.

Right Choices:

Experience is just what happened: life is this very moment, listen to the voices of the moment, you will hear two that are important, what pleases me better please Him (see Psalms 139:7-12).

October 21 – God is Trust

The Bible says, "Early in the morning they left for the Desert of Tekoa. As they set out, Jehoshaphat stood and said, "Listen to me, Judah and people of Jerusalem! Have faith in the LORD your God and you will be upheld; have faith in his prophets and you will be successful" (2Chronicles 20:20).

Trust, as we take steps into life, we acknowledge and seek His presence on the way, not merely asking for His blessing once we have gone our way.

Without God I am:

Trusting, what kind of worked yesterday, I drive my life by looking in the rearview mirror, not realizing the crash ahead about to slay me.

With God I am:

Trusting God to change my life, and create a new outcome by my better choices.

Right Choices:

Trusting God requires faith and hope, for these things have become evident by an everlasting and present God. Invading our lives daily, and knowing He will never leave us. So, the trust and hope continues each new day as ever (see Psalm 40:3).

October 22 – God is Wanting to be Near

The Bible says, "In the same way, the Spirit helps us in our weakness. We do not know what we ought to pray for, but the Spirit himself intercedes for us with groans that words cannot express. 27And he who searches our hearts knows the mind of the Spirit, because the Spirit intercedes for the saints in accordance with God's will" (Romans 8:26-27).

Wanting to be near, the key is not in what we can do to overcome, but rather how we surrender our will to Him and the power and might of God will cause evil to take flight.

Without God I am:

Feeling Despair, I struggled to pretend at times that maybe God did care for me and that He existed as Savior of my life, but something awful pulled me down - back into my strife.

With God I am:

Surrendered, daily to the loving hand of God, this Jesus is powerful and intends only good for me, so patiently I walk to see what He makes of me.

Right Choices:

Nearer my soul to Thee, oh how I feel so free (see 1 Corinthians 9:1)!

OCTOBER 23 – GOD IS RELEASING US

The Bible says, "For even the Son of Man did not come to be served, but to serve, and to give his life as a ransom for many" (Mark 10:45).

Releasing, us from self-judgment, because we laid all our sins at the foot of the cross of Christ, whenever our remembrances come, we simply command our mind to "stop"!

Without God I am:

Released, from a sense of duty to no one, except myself, my wife/husband, family, and job. I have my standards and morals, but there are no absolutes - all is relative.

With God I am:

Released, from the bondage of sin, which Satan disguises so eloquently, this simply means as I surrender my desire for sin and desire more of Him, something joyous is happening within.

Right Choices:

This is a progressive tense word: it is actively at work this moment, it never goes away, and it will not stop until we are one with Him in heaven. We need to be releasing ourselves to Him as He frees us from ourselves (see Romans 8:1).

OCTOBER 24 – GOD IS JEALOUS

The Bible says, "If you forsake the LORD and serve foreign gods, he will turn and bring disaster on you and make an end of you, after he has been good to you" (Joshua 24:20).

Jealous, when we abandon the Giver of all good - our wealth, health, success - crowding our time with work and pleasure, in total indifference to and content without Him. He still loves us.

Without God I am:

Appreciated, by the enemy and friends for how my life seems so carefree and full of good things. Christians look in awe at all that I have and wonder why?

With God I am:

Appreciated, by God when I walk in the shadow (behind) the Glory and Grace of God Almighty, doing His will and acknowledging His amazing power in my life.

Right Choices:

God requires exclusive dominion with no other gods before Him: it's a commandment, one of the ten, the first. So, it's not just important: it's crucial and critical to each (see Nahum 1:2).

October 25 – God is Uniting Us

The Bible says, "The body is a unit, though it is made up of many parts; and though all its parts are many, they form one body. So it is with Christ. 13For we were all baptized by one Spirit into one body--whether Jews or Greeks, slave or free--and we were all given the one Spirit to drink" (1Corinthians 12:12-13).

Uniting us, as brothers and sisters of one global society, bound together by the Holy Spirit of God, whose foundation is love.

Without God I am:

United, with my sense of identity, who I am, how I look, the image I project, my desires, goals, achievements, failures and sometimes laziness.

With God I am:

United, with a God who is intent on achieving something ideal in my life out of all the good, bad, and the ugly.

Right Choices:

God is good, and it all works together for righteousness, what really matters are not only the goals but the process. Seeing and believing the difference He makes in all (see 1 Corinthians 1:10).

October 26 – God is Our Solitude

The Bible says, "Very early in the morning, while it was still dark, Jesus got up, left the house and went off to a solitary place, where he prayed" (Mark 1:35).

Our solitude, in a quiet place, pause and reset our mind, pray for God's Grace and claim His promises for all time. Leave all unclean, unkind, untrue behind, go now with the assurance Jesus is mine.

Without God I am:

Alone, with myself and some not so friendly unseen friends, my thoughts wander over hills of worry, storm clouds are brewing, I feel the rush of a cold breeze, I must go now.

With God I am:

Alone with God, in the stillness of His might, He holds me tight, my fright is gone, I was all wrong for trying to be so strong, His abiding Grace is changing all my wrongs.

Right Choices:

Nothing can calm the craziness in our lives like time alone with God. He's the grease to make the wheels of life role easily. He's the magnum .44 cal gun that keeps the enemy at bay. He's the ruler of the universe who guides the stars and guides me (see - Mark 6:31

OCTOBER 27 – GOD IS OUR CALL CENTER

The Bible says, "Therefore I tell you, whatever you ask for in prayer, believe that you have received it, and it will be yours" (Mark 11:24).

Our Call Center, the prayers never stop coming, His response is always sure, never too late, always right, completely satisfying in the end. But we worry within - oh ye of little faith - walk straight.

Without God I am:

A call center, my day planner at hand, I schedule it tight, every minute counts, it feels good to be needed.

With God I am:

Calling, not out of despair for lack of assurance, but decisions ahead require a clear head. I seek Him in confidence knowing, He will guide my thoughts and steps through each passing day as I pray.

Right Choices:

Call centers are places where companies create central responses for customers who need help. The problem here is if we don't call, nothing changes. Most likely, we get help from places that lack the graces, and it chases us to places, we simply should not go (see Psalm 4:1).

October 28 – God is Unfailing Love

The Bible says, "The LORD loves righteousness and justice; the earth is full of his unfailing love" (Psalm 33:5).

Unfailing love, in the midst of my greatest neglect of God, wrapped up in all the pleasures of the day, held deep in fear and anxiety, not able to think of God, and how He cares for my deepest need.

Without God I am:

Failing, ever to know the true reality of my situation.

With God I am:

Failing, but then remembering His everlasting love, I call on His name to guide and direct my steps.

Right Choices:

Unfailing means never-ending or never falling short, but we ask, "what about all the bad things that happen to good people?", and we look at lost opportunities and bad circumstances. In the end, it's not about me: it's about God and how he uses me to help me and others to see what He wants to be in a time, we can't yet see (see Matthew 22:37).

OCTOBER 29 – GOD IS OUR MENTOR

The Bible says, "Show me your ways, O LORD, teach me your paths; 5guide me in your truth and teach me, for you are God my Savior, and my hope is in you all day long" (Psalms 25:4-5).

Our mentor, teaching us by His Word, His saints, and Holy Spirit. Expectantly we see the difference transforming our lives by His grace and power - our faith grows.

Without God I am:

Mentored, as my mind matures and selectively chooses that which will become my reality.

With God I am:

Mentored, by God to understand the atonement of the cross and what it means for me. The death of all my sin, the victory won, by Him, given freely with only one request. Let this new nature reign daily by the power of redemption.

Right Choices:

The thing about mentoring is this; we need to have a teachable spirit, be willing to be transformed, yielding, not selectively picking and choosing that which will be. But all in, given to what it would make of me (see Isaiah 9:6).

October 30 – God is Alone

The Bible says, "So they went away by themselves in a boat to a solitary place" (Mark 6:32).

Alone, in the oneness of His love - hope and courage, He comes to our loneliness, wrapping it with the comfort, and assurance of His strength and might.

Without God I am:

Wrapped up, in my world, the job, spouse, mate, kids, making and spending money, if I only had the view of You – what else would I do.

With God I am:

Wrapped up, in a bigger world, it's a challenge to put it on pause and remember my cause, I am going through the motions way too much with all my emotions.

Right Choices:

This is not a group date, not a business meeting, not a show. We're not in a group setting with a conference agenda: this is Him and me, deep within, nothing hidden for He knows it all anyway, so He ministers to me. Think about ministering to Him, deep within, giving Him today all my sin, letting it go, turning from it, we put a smile on His face when we do - keep Him smiling (see Psalm 136:4).

October 31 – God is Ready

The Bible says, "And we know that in all things God works for the good of those who love him, who have been called according to his purpose" (Romans 8:28).

Ready, always to put things in motion. We just need to get used to the notion, He's driving - I'm riding, He's writing - I'm reading, He's feeding - I'm nourished, He's coming - I'm going to a better place.

Without God I am:

Ready, to condemn God for how He allows bad things to happen to good people.

With God I am:

Ready, to understand that the physical world and the spiritual world are two separate entities. What happens in one does not determine action in the other – but God works all things to His Glory.

Right Choices:

Ready or not here I come (see Matthew 24:44)!

November 1 – God is Grieved

The Bible says, "Because of the LORD's great love we are not consumed, for his compassions never fail" (Lamentations 3:22).

Grieved, when pain ravages our body, physical or emotional loss cripples us, and we rush through each gifted day and forget to pray.

Without God I am:

Grieved, by my sorrow, hurt, and pain when I look in vain and try to refrain from doing those things that hurt me and others most.

With God I am:

Grieved, that I could not believe, but relieved - knowing that God never gives up on me.

Right Choices:

Grieved means to cause to be with deep sadness, it's usually about lost blessings from God (see Psalm 95:10).

NOVEMBER 2 – GOD IS SPEAKING

The Bible says, "For since the creation of the world God's invisible qualities--his eternal power and divine nature--have been clearly seen, being understood from
what has been made, so that men are without excuse" (Romans 1:20).

Speaking, to our soul when we gaze upon a crimson sunset, enjoy the bouquet of hills filled with autumn's golden splendid color. He quiets our screaming indifference, assuring His presence is near.

Without God I am:

Speaking, and looking for assurance from many sources, none of which seem to have any ultimate authority - I run a legal life.

With God I am:

Speaking, and listening as one who is taught by God, from His Word and Holy Spirit. The revelation of God has been made known in the Bible.

Right Choices:

The living word (Bible) is God-breathed, powerful, life-changing, visible, and invisible reality. It is enduring the greatest skeptic with lasting records, as the best seller of all time. Let ten minutes a day be like feeding the five thousand with five small fish (see Numbers 7:89).

November 3 – God is Opening Our Minds

The Bible says, "Blessed are they who keep his statutes and seek him with all their heart" (Psalm 119:2).

Opening our minds, to understand scripture, and through His Holy Spirit as we study His word, empowering our lives to be His people.

Without God I am:

Opening, myself up to the vast array of influences, all of which compete for my allegiance. In the end, I claim only for myself will, which is taking me over the hill.

With God I am:

Opening, myself up to a vast array of influences, I set my standards on biblical truth and use these to determine and test my allegiance.

Right Choices:

Opening my mind to think that as obedience takes hold, as a result of doing what I was told, while letting Him mold, with values as good as gold (see Isaiah 42:20).

November 4 – God is Quality of Life

The Bible says, "In him was life, and that life was the light of men. 5The light shines in the darkness, but the darkness has not understood it" (John 1:4).

Quality of life, for what is quality but conformance to requirements, the key here remains, God's or mine, let there be no doubt what this is all about.

Without God I am:

Qualified, in my daily destiny of positioning my requirements alongside my actions, the results are good so I must be doing what I should.

With God I am:

Qualified, to be the greatest sinner of all time, tis but grace had a better place for this face to shine, making my time - count as Thine.

Right Choices:

The thing about quality is that it is pervasive, to be real, it is endless and everlasting. It goes to the depth of the core of all that it is, you just know it when you see it and experience it - it's real, not only smells good, it is good (see Psalm 27:1).

November 5 – God is Bathing Our Spirit

The Bible says, "If you remain in me and my words remain in you, ask whatever you wish, and it will be given you" (John 15:7).

Bathing our spirit, with a calm balm, the best rest, strength that has length, courage to flourish, and hope with a note of gladness and cheer.

Without God I am:

Bathed, in the muddy water of all my sin, I never get clean.

With God I am:

Bathed, in the glory and majesty of a triumphant God, I take His rod to fight against all the odds - all the other gods.

Right Choices:

This is about as big an "If," as you can imagine. The key here is, in whom are we remaining? Is it myself or my divine partner (see Acts 3:20).

November 6 – God is Taking Our Discontentment

The Bible says, "Moreover, when God gives any man wealth and possessions, and enables him to enjoy them, to accept his lot and be happy in his work--this is a gift of God" (Ecclesiastes 5:19).

Taking our discontentment, with life in this physical world, our lack of resources, poorer conditions, wants beyond means, and unfilled dreams and giving us a thankful heart to start.

Without God I am:

Discontented, with how so many "things" seem to content me so little, the prize I seek keeps getting bigger each time I trigger the start of something bigger.

With God I am:

Content, only in the knowledge that I measure my satisfaction by my appetite to delight myself, but God measures it by my hunger to be right with Him.

Right Choices:

It's OK to be discontent with my knowledge of a loving God, that's about it. He will gladly take that and give you something you never imagined possible (see 1 Samuel 22:2).

November 7 – God is Returning

The Bible says, "if my people, who are called by my name, will humble themselves and pray and seek my face and turn from their wicked ways, then will I hear from heaven and will forgive their sin and will heal their land" (2Chronicles 7:14).

Returning, to our repeated sin to forgive again, He takes our regrets and helps us forget, our shame dies with all of Satan's lies. We go better now to help others defeat our foe.

Without God I am:

Going, to my sin again to feed a hunger deep within, which knows no limits, and consumes all my precious minutes.

With God I am:

Going, back to old failures and temptations, for Satan has no new tricks. He gets his kicks from seeing me pick, those lies before my eyes, yet come Lord Jesus to renew, my new beginning too.

Right Choices:

Another "if" statement, beware of these. It starts by getting on our knees and humbly asking God to change how we think and give us a new perspective about what good really lies in that broken path of thinking errors (see Isaiah 30:15).

November 8 – God is Empowering Us

The Bible says, "Let the word of Christ dwell in you richly as you teach and admonish one another with all wisdom, and as you sing psalms, hymns and spiritual songs with gratitude in your hearts to God" (Colossians 3:16).

Empowering us, through His abiding Holy Spirit, the essence of God. Like a drop of dye it changes the color of our life, our selfish greed is taught to nourish others; we flourish with a Holy fragrance.

Without God I am:

Empowered, with engines of greed, I seek to believe, that my ultimate good, is all that should - really matter.

With God I am:

Empowered, with the creator Himself, through His work in my life. I progress as faith creates knowledge, which builds understanding, and belief creates reverence, which creates wisdom and love.

Right Choices:

Are you feeling like He is nowhere around to help, the enemy is calling, the temptation is rising, and sweet sin is calling, what shall I do? Keep moving, whatever you do, don't stop, keep getting closer to Him, not to sin (see 1 Corinthians 12:6).

November 9 – God is Giving Us New Beginnings

The Bible says, "But the angel said to them, "Do not be afraid. I bring you good news of great joy that will be for all the people. 11Today in the town of David a Savior has been born to you; he is Christ the Lord" (Luke 2:10-11).

Giving us new beginnings, our perseverance begins each day with a clean slate, praise God from whom all blessings flow, God - give us a thankful heart today as we pray.

Without God I am:

Starting over, to build that compartment wall thicker, where I put all my grief and sorrow - guilt and shame, Jesus came to take all the blame, His pain freed my name - now claim His title - Savior.

With God I am:

Starting anew, each day as I pray - with a thankful heart, the world makes me anxious at the start, but my God is here to help me steer, clear of every fear.

Right Choices:

This is the most significant new beginning of all time, the new covenant - Christ! Can we call God a failure? No, he proved His point by showing us a man without God is hopeless (see 1 John 2:7).

November 10 – God is Our Witness

The Bible says, "But you will receive power when the Holy Spirit comes on you; and you will be my witnesses in Jerusalem, and in all Judea and Samaria, and to the ends of the earth" (Acts 1:8).

Our witness, yet we tremble to speak His name to a friend, share a prayer, ask a blessing for a meal, and so people wonder if our faith is real.

Without God I am:

Witnessing, daily by my lifestyle and actions, the values and morals that set me apart - I want people to see the good
in me.

With God I am:

Witnessing, daily by my life style and actions, the values and morals that set me apart - I want people to see Jesus
in me.

Right Choices:

Witness means to make a statement regarding the truth of something. If you can't tell anybody else, tell the Lord today how much you appreciate Him being near (see Hebrews 12:1).

November 11 – God is Alive

The Bible says, "In the same way, count yourselves dead to sin but alive to God in Christ Jesus. 12Therefore do not let sin reign in your mortal body so that you obey its evil desires" (Romans 6:11-12).

Alive, bringing courage where fear is near, casting hope upon despair, building faith through obedience, changing lives by destroying Satan's lies.

Without God I am:

Alive, and able to make a new choice, for the final day, has not yet come when judgment will condemn, this soul to a dark role.

With God I am:

Alive, in Christ - now rest on His promise, that He will never leave me or forsake me and wants only good for me - His unconditional love for me is immense.

Right Choices:

Alive and available, you say, but I'm not seeing or feeling it, it's distant, dull, dead, and done with me - not so fast. He's just a prayer away, but even nearer so, steer clear of Sheol (see 1 Peter 3:18).

November 12 – God is Correcting Thinking Errors

The Bible says, "Brothers, stop thinking like children. In regard to evil be infants, but in your thinking be adults" (1Corinthians 14:20).

Correcting thinking errors, we keep getting more of what we have but don't want when we keep doing the wrong things, God sets our minds in rhythm with Him in His Word.

Without God I am:

Thinking wrong, about what is right and wrong, my morals are relative. God sent His Son to atone alone, once and for all, the perfect sacrifice for this life. Now it's my turn to give it back.

With God I am:

Thinking, it's my turn now to give this life to Christ as He gave His life for me, living obediently for Him to see His life in me.

Right Choices:

Correcting means changing the wrong things and making them right. They say attitude is altitude, and heaven is a very high place, cultivate right thinking by thinking WWJD "What Would Jesus Do" (see 2 Timothy 2:25).

November 13 – God is Bread of Life

The Bible says, "I tell you the truth, he who believes has everlasting life. 48I am the bread of life" (John 6:47-48).

Bread of life, when I realize His timing is perfect and His ultimate plan is right. Surrendering my feeding and seeding
to His kneading of my life removes strife.

Without God I am:

Nourished, by the adrenaline in the hurry of my worry, the flurry of assignments on my plate - don't be late, oh, where can I escape this fate?

With God I am:

Nourished, by a simple faith that walks and talks with Him, I don't give in to the sin. I want more of His goodness, its effect makes me feel right in His sight.

Right Choices:

What do we feed on to have life, usually food, so what food are we talking about here? The food of God is humble pie, fruit of the spirit, Holy Communion - the body and blood of the sacrificial lamb (see John 6:22).

November 14 – God is Taking Our Darkness

The Bible says, "For you were once darkness, but now you are light in the Lord. Live as children of light 9 for the fruit of the light consists in all goodness, righteousness and truth" (Ephesians 5:8-9).

Taking our darkness, as we surrender to Him and let it go, our desires flow as we go in tow to light with this loving and graceful God.

Without God I am:

In darkness, I can't see the wrong for my eyes are blind, as Satan stands to shadow my soul in darkness, but God has written on my heart all I need to know to start - loving Him.

With God I am:

In the light, I know when it's bright, my heart is glad to be walking right, continually in His sight.

Right Choices:

Where do you think He is taking it? Absolutely nowhere, for His light simply destroys darkness, and it is no more, in thought word or deed – it is gone, let His light shine (see Psalm 18:28)!

November 15 – God is A Perfect Builder

The Bible says, "I will listen to what God the LORD will say; he promises peace to his people, his saints-- but let them not return to folly" (Psalm 85:8).

A perfect builder, Jesus develops our mind to be sublime, He puts our heart on the right cart, the wheels of our lives are on His heels, this man/woman/child of God is becoming a saint.

Without God I am:

A builder, using all too often the tools of life incorrectly, I never quite learned how to discern what is really right and wrong.

With God I am:

Building, my life on the foundation "rock" of Jesus Christ, whose building plan is revealed totally in the Bible.

Right Choices:

How about being stamped with "Made by the Hand of God" in His Kingdom! Wear it well, my fellow saint, let the tag show (see Psalm 118:22).

November 16 – God is Making Us Precious

The Bible says, "He will rescue them from oppression and violence, for precious is their blood in his sight" (Psalm 72:14).

Making us precious, in His sight for He sees a willing soul made strong by His might, our battle scars the sin that marred, a fragile heart now tended and mended by a gracious God.

Without God I am:

Precious, still in His sight, He wants me, still cares for me and puts people and "panels" in my path, calling me to my real home abiding with Jesus who came to atone.

With God I am:

Precious, for God, doesn't make junk, a unique one of a kind miracle, with the handprint of God almighty on my soul.

Right Choices:

When something is precious, it has special meaning, and we take special care of it. I often just feel like another face taking up space, but God has grace, keeping pace with my race, it's His way of keeping us from going astray (see Isaiah 43:4).

NOVEMBER 17 – GOD IS TURNING OUR LIABILITIES

The Bible says, "they will eat the fruit of their ways and be filled with the fruit of their schemes. 32For the waywardness of the simple will kill them, and the complacency of fools will destroy them; 33but whoever listens to me will live in safety and be at ease, without fear of harm" (Proverbs 1:31-33).

Turning our liabilities into assets while our conditional failings were not planned by God. He weaves the strength of character and goodness back into our life from all the strife.

Without God I am:

Turning, over the soil of my life, exposing each new day as a bad flavor of my ways. In how and what I say. My heart has become numb - to the Son.

With God I am:

Turning, assets into eternal fruit, the harvest happens as I make available my life, with care and love I go with Him in obedience.

Right Choices:

Fruit of schemes gone wrong from foolish thoughts that seemed so strong, killing selves with complacent lies of disbelief, but safety lingers for those who hear and fear (see Proverbs 1:7).

November 18 – God is Showing Us

The Bible says, "But man, despite his riches, does not endure; he is like the beasts that perish. 13This is the fate of those who trust in themselves, and of their followers, who approve their sayings" (Psalms 49:12-13).

Showing us, it's not about how moral, decent, or how good we are. It's about accepting the fallen state of man, his inherited badness, and sinfulness and the need for a Savior.

Without God I am:

Fallen, just look around, what are the sounds of a man? Not always but often they are anger, greed, pride, resentment, selfishness, lust, misplaced passion, fear, and mental anxiety. We just keep falling.

With God I am:

Risen, with Christ - granted a new life which sounds like – love compassion, caring, friendship, patience, kindness, sharing, humility, happiness, and serving. We just keep rising.

Right Choices:

Why can't we trust ourselves? I have taken me down a long road, I've traveled to so many places, won so many races, I love me! That is the problem, you see (see Isaiah 13:11)!

November 19 – God is Yours

The Bible says, "My son,' the father said, 'you are always with me, and everything I have is yours" (Luke 15:31).

Yours, for the asking, come into our heart, mind, and soul Lord Jesus, He stands at the door of our life knocking -
moment by moment.

Without God I am:

Mine, but God has a better plan - really grand, but I believe the lies that Satan lays before my eyes.

With God I am:

His, giving my life as I stand beside the plan, ready and willing to be used of Him to bring others in and away
from sin.

Right Choices:

This is not about partnership but ownership. This is a big deal, you'll never see his face this side of eternity, no one ever has, but be glad. He paid for the full meal, now lay hold of the new Sonship and seal. One more thought, it's non-negotiable, you give up everything, but you get to keep all that was ever worth anything (see Luke 10:27).

November 20 – God is Our Answer

The Bible says, "See, he is puffed up; his desires are not upright-- but the righteous will live by his faith" (Habakkuk 2:4).

Our answer, when our soul is cold with anxiety, our worries drown our hope. May our prayers be a rope, to lift us up to sip the cup of His eternal goodness, - filling us with His loving-kindness and hope.

Without God I am:

Answering, my own questions with the results of my hand, which are really grand, I have no need to plead, my case is won - forget the Son.

With God I am:

Answering, my daily need for guidance on bended knee, with prayers of adoration, confession, thanksgiving and petition. Expectantly and patiently, I wait to see God create my fate.

Right Choices:

We tend to look for questions that we like to answer. Today is always ready to borrow from tomorrow's fears. My uncertainty is always ahead of my sight, come Lord Jesus, and give me might to stay in this fight (see 1 John 2:16).

November 21 – God is Our Means

The Bible says, "You open your hand and satisfy the desires of every living thing" (Psalm 145:16).

Our means, all too often to our ways, forgive us Lord.

Without God I am:

My means, and I am blessed, the question remains - by whom and for what.

With God I am:

His means, for here, I stand giving my life to the use of His plan.

Right Choices:

Means is the method by which we achieve our way. It's hard when we don't really know where we are going and what we really need. It seems at times I need so much, and other times, I need so little. The Bible says, God wants to take me to a good place and has an excellent plan. That sounds good, but what I see are waves of desperation and doubt. I don't want to move. Here is the key I see, wait on the Lord by walking with the Lord, in His strength, not mine (see 1 Corinthians 9:22).

November 22 – God is Committed

The Bible says, "And God is able to make all grace abound to you, so that in all things at all times, having all that you need, you will abound in every good work" (2Corinthians 9:8).

Committed, to our constant wavering and doubt, He wants to shout out what He's all about, and so He sends a friend, a sunrise, and or blue skies to raise-up our eyes.

Without God I am:

Committed, to the relentless pursuit of my happiness, but when I get more, I seem to have less, I must confess.

With God I am:

Committed, to the here and now, but God wants me to point this plow, to a horizon gone from now, forgetting the how.

Right Choices:

Some of us decide to engage, it has all the window dressing of commitment. God decided He needed to send His only begotten Son, to die for me. Then, He sent His Holy Spirit to live within me to be an ever-present living reality in my life. How committed is that? This is not all, He's making a heavenly place for me at the end of this race, committed (see Jeremiah 20:12).

November 23 – God is Unafraid

The Bible says, "Mightier than the thunder of the great waters, mightier than the breakers of the sea-- the LORD on high is mighty" (Psalm 93:4).

Not afraid, like we are to face the things that need to change, we've grown accustomed to our status, but God offers gratis, and says "come-on", I'll carry you beyond this pond.

Without God I am:

Afraid, that around the next bend, the road will end, with no place to go, I'll face the foe, oh my soul, come now Jesus as He pleases, and save this weary soul.

With God I am:

Afraid, to let go of the show, Lord Jesus help me to know that where I stand is part of your plan - if not, move me gently.

Right Choices:

God is unafraid to move me to places where I don't want to go, because it helps build trust and faith in knowing it was only He that enabled my success. Like the valley of the shadow of death, we will fear no evil, for His rod and staff will comfort us, which simply is the power of God (see Joshua 10:8)!

November 24 – God is Beautiful

The Bible says, "One thing I ask of the LORD, this is what I seek: that I may dwell in the house of the LORD all the days of my life, to gaze upon the beauty of the LORD and to seek Him in his temple" (Psalm 27:4).

Beautiful, made so by His holiness, while sin makes people ugly - ruthless - and forlorn, through our sanctification, we become treasures of gold as we unfold.

Without God I am:

Skin deep, with beauty that will not last, God says He will burn- up the things of our life that have no eternal value.

With God I am:

Beautiful, how His holiness has cleansed my life and given me a wellspring of desire and love to serve others.

Right Choices:

What makes something beautiful, how do we define it? We don't, it just is. We know it when we see it. So it is with God, reflected in the beauty of His creation, landscapes, birds, flowers, animals, and you and me (see Ecclesiastes 3:11).

November 25 – God is Not Indifferent

The Bible says, "For the waywardness of the simple will kill them, and the complacency of fools will destroy them" (Proverbs 1:32).

Not indifferent, to our needs as one whose witness is our Existence. In a created world of order and beauty, the details of our life now matter most to Him, especially our sin.

Without God I am:

Indifferent, to God but He is still there, to care and tend this life, ignored not by God because this life is precious - for He died for all alike.

With God I am:

Not indifferent, to the sin that rages within, but is not acted out, because God has helped me to see what I'm all about.

Right Choices:

Indifferent means having little regard for the importance of something to me. God never has this attitude toward me, while often I do of Him. It happens when things are good, and I'm well most often. I fail to see the blessings from Thee, keeping myself on bended knee (see Isaiah 2:17).

November 26 – God is Timely

The Bible says, "And God is able to make all grace abound to you, so that in all things at all times, having all that you need, you will abound in every good work" (2Corinthians 9:8).

Timely, never late - never early, things happen as surely, as
He knows they must, now trust and don't fuss. His timing
runs on obedience, patience, and trust.

Without God I am:

Timely, about tending to my needs, no price too high, as long as I, can see a means to my ends.

With God I am:

Timely, about worry and being anxious for today, now did I
pray about this day? - or say… "let's go this way anyway."

Right Choices:

What's my engine running on? I all too often run on pride, self-determination, discipline to the cause, and routine. So, how is it working for me? It may be right, but time is not on my side, this engine will slide and glide to places where it wants to hide. May grace abound for my willful negligence, today - take a second look at His book (see 2 Corinthians 4:15).

November 27 – God is To Be Accepted

The Bible says, "This is good, and pleases God our Savior, 4who wants all men to be saved and to come to a knowledge of the truth. 5For there is one God and one mediator between God and men, the man Christ Jesus, 6who gave himself as a ransom for all men--the testimony given in its proper time" (1Timothy 2:3-6).

To be accepted, and taken as a gift from above, His love to meld our heart, gives us a new start, each day as we pray.

Without God I am:

Taking, my emotions into each new day, I compare my life to others in strife and think "things are good," so I tend to befriend the source of the force.

With God I am:

Accepting, my forgiven sin, as the mortar that rebuilds the blocks of my character, in the end, God's a friend who made me whole and restored my soul.

Right Choices:

The hardest thing about a gift is accepting it. Why is this? Most often, I don't want to be beholden to anyone, just myself. It creates an expectation for me to do the same in my mind. I don't want to go there, be willing today (see 2 Corinthians 6:2).

November 28 – God is Going To Do

The Bible says, "Give thanks to the LORD, for he is good; his love endures forever" (Psalm 118:1).
Going to do – as He ought to, to make me more of what the original plan called for.
Without God I am:

Going to do, what I want to, and in the end - it will offend.

With God I am:

Going to be, what He wants me to be, so He and others can see Himself in me.
Right Choices:

There is a mystery here in all of it, doing. I watched a bird the other morning outside my window. It was moving from branch to branch continuously, going, looking for food, knowing what it needed was just a hop away. In prayer, when I draw near to the tank of the wellspring of life, God is doing what I need most, and He's just a prayer away (see Exodus 15:11).

November 29 – God is Going Along

The Bible says, "No temptation has seized you except what is common to man. And God is faithful; he will not let you be tempted beyond what you can bear. But when you are tempted, he will also provide a way out so that you can stand up under it" (1Corinthians 10:13).

Going with us, but I want to feel alone - thinking I'm free
to be me, but that's the real problem you see.

Without God I am:

Going alone, thinking of my choices, I place them in rooms of my mind, never to enter again. I feel separated from the deed done. If I could only know the damage done.

With God I am:

Going together, unloading my cares, worries, doubts, temptation knocks, but the "Rock" blocks, my desire to act out, and heaven shouts -Glory to God in the highest.

Right Choices:

The way out for me sometimes is to give in to my sin. Deep within motivations work that remains uncharted ground for redemptions work. God's provision and my restoration are out of sync. Be ready to form the link and let God tend to this kink (see Ezekiel 1:21).

November 30 – God is Growing Us Up

The Bible says, "The unfolding of your words gives light; it gives understanding to the simple" (Psalm 119:130).

Growing us up, enlightening our hearts, feeling a fresh start, victories small. Still, we stand tall, one at a time growing just fine, our joy is coming back, as we value more now His protection from attack.

Without God I am:

Growing, to like more and more in how I keep score, me everything, them nothing, well maybe not that bad, but what is for real? I feel this makes sense because I'm real.

With God I am:

Growing in Christ, my mind is renewed, to see a fresh perspective now blessed, with holy eyes that prize a gracious God going with me to grow me up.

Right Choices:

The hardest thing about growing up is wanting to stay young. We think only a few things get better with age, wine, green bananas, memories of my youth, and old friends. Unfolding words from His Book are like tender morsels that give life, bring hope, and strengthen faith (see Mark 4:8).

December 1 – God is Distressed

The Bible says, "In all their distress he too was distressed, and the angel of his presence saved them. In his love and mercy he redeemed them; he lifted them up and carried them all the days of old" (saiah 63:9).

Distressed, at all the injustice in the world, people persecuted for worshiping Him, starvation, killing, and our indifference for not wanting to make a difference.

Without God I am:

Distressed, by just about anything, that money can't fix, but I stuff it and go about having my kicks.

With God I am:

Distressed, when I long for an answer to prayer, that just doesn't seem to be there, I wonder if He cares, as I stare into the air.

Right Choices:

I'm distressed as is God at the shallowness of my convictions and beliefs. Too many of us just don't seem to get it. Why is it so complicated? God says His yoke is light. There is still too much of me in this puzzle, and not enough of Him, can't seem to let Him in, need to pray again (see Mark 14:33).

December 2 – God is Wanting My All

The Bible says, "Now if you obey me fully and keep my covenant, then out of all nations you will be my treasured possession. Although the whole earth is mine, 6you will be for me a kingdom of priests and a holy nation" (Exodus 19:5-6).

Wanting my all, but I crave for just a little bit of bad, but the bits make their hits, desire rushes in for a bigger score, Satan's laughing at my door, at my grief which atop he sits.

Without God I am:

Wanting, more of what I don't have, I hope it will fill the hole in my desire, my happiness is rolling on four flat tires.

With God I am:

Wanting, to be free of the lust in me, thinking errors that drive passions afoul, but if I throw in the towel, one step down a wrong road will never get me to the right place.

Right Choices:

When I think about how much is my all, it comes down to one simple thing - when I dishonor the Lord, confess it immediately, and pray for more of Him and less of me (see Proverbs 18:3).

December 3 – God is Bringing Us To Terms

The Bible says, "This then is how we know that we belong to the truth, and how we set our hearts at rest in his presence 20whenever our hearts condemn us. For God is greater than our hearts, and he knows everything" (1John 3:18-20).

Bringing us to terms, with our present condition and situation, our flesh screams for control and more, while Christ opens the door to pour Himself and Spirit galore unto our life if we adore - Him.

Without God I am:

Coming to terms, with the condition of my decisions. Greed is my steed, pride is my ride - step aside.

With God I am:

Learning the terms, and conditions of my situation. My value to Him is how I bring myself in surrender as a slave to Him as a friend.

Right Choices:

The point is the terms are all His. The deal is pretty clear, He paid the price, so what is it going to cost me? Just about everything this sinful mortal body ever wanted, except my free will, be all in (see Psalm 109:21).

December 4 – God is A Perfect Rest

The Bible says, "Behold, I am coming soon! My reward is with me, and I will give to everyone according to what he has done" (Revelation 22:12).

A perfect rest, when we have withstood the test, made the right choice, we hear His voice, calling come and enjoy my company and your reward.

Without God I am:

Restless, trying to get by with less, when more pushed me out of control through too many doors, I need some rest.

With God I am:

Restful, what a friend I have in Jesus, I plan my ways, but He directs my steps, moving me, and using me to be free.

Right Choices:

I wonder what He is going to give. It's like looking under the Christmas tree at all the presents and wondering which one is for me. My Dad used to switch names on the presents, I wonder if God will do that? Will I be disappointed? Oh, for the grace of God, how wonderful and beautiful is His name (see 2 Corinthians 12:9)!

December 5 – God is Pardoning Grace

The Bible says, "He who conceals his sins does not prosper, but whoever confesses and renounces them finds mercy" (Proverbs 28:13).

Pardoning grace, He looks us in the face, and sees now our redeemed forgiven place, our robes white as snow, as we go in the grace of almighty God.

Without God I am:

Stuck, with getting more of what I don't need or want because I keep doing the same things I wish I hadn't.

With God I am:

Pardoned, to realize my acceptance is only contingent on my reception of the living Son's death on the cross for all my iniquity. His enabling grace and mercy will guide and empower my choices over the temptation to sin – daily.

Right Choices:

Ever feel like you had two arms tied behind your back fighting all these demons? I'm my own worst enemy. I think God thinks so. He smiles and thinks, OK, this guy needs a break - angels...cut him some slack, throw him a rope, and take him in tow. Ah....the fresh breeze of redemption is back, thank you Jesus (see 1 Corinthians 1:4)!

December 6 – God is Making All Things New

The Bible says, "Therefore, if anyone is in Christ, he is a new creation; the old has gone, the new has come" (2 Corinthians 5:17)!

Making all things new, from the inside out, it's simply what He's all about, so give a shout! - and don't drop out,

Without God I am:

Making, most things conditional, there is nothing here original, except my fallen state, my sin makes Satan grin.

With God I am:

Making, all things right in His sight, pride, and ego in check, God stacks the deck, making Satan a wreck!

Right Choices:

I'm going to call it, another "if" statement, watch out for these! I feel way too often like an old creation, and the old has come, and the new is in a holding pattern. I like the idea of making Satan a wreck, doesn't sound possible, but help is just a prayer away, and that has to make Satan a wreck (see 2Corinthians 4:16).

December 7 – God is Creating Significance

The Bible says, "For by him all things were created: things in heaven and on earth, visible and invisible, whether thrones or powers or rulers or authorities; all things were created by him and for him" (Colossians 1:16).

Creating significance, out of our silence alone in a room, He comes soon, opening our mind to refine how we dine on this gracious gifted life - so fine.

Without God I am:

Creating, a will that will overfill, on just about anything that pleases me well, it's not a matter if whether - but only that I could.

With God I am:

Creating, a destiny of eternal value, the trail from earth to Heaven is full of divine appointments.

Right Choices:

So, where do we take this from here? Hard to see how easy it is at times to be really free. The significance I seek is often wrong, it's not about me. It's about letting an amazing God use me to set myself and others free. To love, to worship, to be what He initially intended me to be, free from the bondage of sin (see Galatians 5:1)!

December 8 – God is Challenging Us

The Bible says, "Blessed are the pure in heart, for they will see God. 9Blessed are the peacemakers, for they will be called sons of God. 10Blessed are those who are persecuted because of righteousness, for theirs is the kingdom of heaven" (Matthew 5:8-10).

Challenging us, to follow Him and not give in, Satan slips us lies if we think through our eyes, Christ will show us the way to a better day.

Without God I am:

Challenged, to revel in the pursuit of solutions, glory is mine as I refine how things should be, this world - this life would all be fine, with enough good thinking from my mind.

With God I am:

Challenged, to realize that my inherent nature is full of all the wrong motives, renewed by His grace, I claim new ground, found wanting to turn around - but God keeps me sound.

Right Choices:

God is not only challenging us, He is enabling us. Pure in heart, what does that mean? We say he has a good heart. Most often, it means God is on his side, and he is on God's (see 1 Timothy 1:12).

December 9 – God is Finished

The Bible says, "When he had received the drink, Jesus said, "It is finished." With that, he bowed his head and gave up his spirit" (John 19:30).

Finished, His work done for all mankind, yet blind we toil to make His deathless love mine, "come now" He says and surrender as slave, letting all our sin fall to the grave of Christ - unseen, gone, - past, present, future - clean.

Without God I am:

Finished, but yet just one thought, one step away from a better day, stop - look - and listen, if I would just think to pray, "God help me today".

With God I am:

Finished, trying to fight each sinful battle alone, I put on the full armor of God to protect and fight for what is right, God almighty is by my side - we're going for a mighty ride.

Right Choices:

The last thing Jesus did on this earth was take a drink and say it was finished. Not just a good finish, an amazing finish. He gave it up. What He had come to do, He did. What was it? He gave us a way out of this mess, if we confess. All we need to realize is that we need it, and Him (see Hebrews 4:3).

December 10 – God is Purity

The Bible says, "The precepts of the LORD are right, giving joy to the heart. The commands of the LORD are radiant, giving light to the eyes. 9The fear of the LORD is pure, enduring forever. The ordinances of the LORD are sure and altogether righteous" (Psalms 19:8-9).

Purity, His intent has no stint of greed, fear, lust, pride, or unfaithful deed. Nobly and humbly He stands, as the almighty and alorious, I Am, offering His hand to each man-women-child.

Without God I am:

Pure, in my own intent to not relent, my will for the Lord to fill, my heart with a new start.

With God I am:

Pure, in my own intent to relent, to become the person God has uniquely created me to be, His workmanship to serve others in love - God's glory be!

Right Choices:

A long way from purity, but I'm on the road. It's a town up ahead, not just in my head, but my heart too. It's filled with all the right stuff, no crime, lots of work to do, friendly folk, all willing to help me along to settle down (see 2 Corinthians 6:6).

December 11 – God is Dethroning Us

The Bible says, "Put to death, therefore, whatever belongs to your earthly nature: sexual immorality, impurity, lust, evil desires and greed, which is idolatry. 6Because of these, the wrath of God is coming" (Colossians 3:5-6).

Dethroning us, taking our self assertions, putting Christ at the center of our wills, to kill the ego and pride that fills our ills. Lord, make our desire to be inspired by your Holy Spirit.

Without God I am:

Enthroned, with total self-absorption, hell will be like this, thinking daily about nothing other than my despair, oh to see now a God who cares.

With God I am:

Enthroned, with the battle of wills, this God of mine fills me with a peace that self-assertion will never reach, take the parade of all my "stuff," and set me free to be like Thee.

Right Choices:

It's a solid throne, reaching way beyond my means. I'm clinging to it because I built it, like all the idols of the Old Testament, they're my gods. It's neat to worship me. I make the rules and always win, but I'm playing a game of shame (see Isaiah 10:13).

December 12 – God is Our Silence

The Bible says, "equip you with everything good for doing his will, and may he work in us what is pleasing to him, through Jesus Christ, to whom be glory forever and ever. Amen" (Hebrews 13:21).

Our silence, in a still moment of a peaceful mind, God quiets my raging life to find, whispers from His heart to mine, trust Him, have courage, be humble, and it will all be just fine.

Without God I am:

Silenced, by the deafening noise of my life, I look for "signs" in all the wrong places. I want to be "spiritual", it gives me a sense that something is good under this hood.

With God I am:

Silenced, by God to stop the clamor of my day, to pray and say, hey, praise God! I love you, Jesus, thank you for today, take my fear and anxiety and give me hope. Oh, how He loves to please you and me!

Right Choices:

I am pleasing to Him, what a neat thought. To think that I could begin to do anything that would "please" the God of the universe is almost absurd, but it's true, He said it (see Proverbs 16:7).

December 13 – God is Full Hearted

The Bible says, "For the wages of sin is death, but the gift of God is eternal life in Christ Jesus our Lord" (Romans 6:23).

Full hearted, His purpose is sure, meant for our life to be pure, this life a precious gift from Him, thank you, Jesus, and now we gift it back to win, a greater gift to be free from the bondage of sin.

Without God I am:

Half hearted, single minded about my spiritual essence, it leads me to sit atop this fence, not sure what I believe. I've decided now to never leave this lofty nest where I rest.

With God I am:

Half hearted, double-minded about who I am in Christ, my soul screams for a non-complacent role, so hitch each day to Him as I pray, God, please give me courage and a willing heart to be your slave today.

Right Choices:

Full hearted in that He made me, knows all my weaknesses and the sins that drag me away. So grab hold of today and let Him leverage the sway towards holiness (see Hebrews 11:6).

December 14 – God is Buoyancy

The Bible says, "Away from me, all you who do evil, for the LORD has heard my weeping. 9The LORD has heard my cry for mercy; the LORD accepts my prayer. 10All my enemies will be ashamed and dismayed; they will turn back in sudden disgrace" (Psalms 6:8-10).

Buoyancy, enabling my life to float above the debris, His grace comes onto me, so I'm free to see how much better His way will be.

Without God I am:

Buoyant, for the moment, I kick hard to stay a-float. I feel too often, "this is all she wrote." I'm about ready to give up if only I could look up and see what God sees, me, a child of His love.

With God I am:

Buoyant, wrapped in a life vest of God's grace, His mercies ever-flowing and new every morning. I keep growing, fixing my eyes not on the debris, but on His desire for my purity.

Right Choices:

The nice thing about buoyancy is we get to keep our head above the water. This allows sight, breath, a sense that I'm able to navigate life and keep on with the fight (see 2 Corinthians 1:10).

December 15 – God is Un-crowded

The Bible says, "I will walk about in freedom, for I have sought out your precepts" (Psalm 119:45).

Un-crowded, His space for me is always free, coming now as I request of Thee, giving me a sense and awareness of Thee, Oh Lord Jesus forgive me for forgetting Thee.

Without God I am:

Crowded, in that we can only think of one thing at a time, and believe me, my mind rarely finds time to think about the "signs" of the times and the wall growing taller where my ladder leans.

With God I am:

Crowded, so much of my time is focused on me and not on Thee, forgive me, Lord, for thinking that I would be better, at last, to blaze a trail fast, going ahead and not being led by you.

Right Choices:

His space is un-crowded because few find it or want it. The space is not crazy jam-packed with demands that cannot be met, but simply a place where lovers go, to be awed by the simplicity of His love, mercy, and grace (see Zephaniah 3:8).

December 16 – God is Washing This Vessel

The Bible says, "Come near to God and he will come near to you. Wash your hands, you sinners, and purify your hearts, you double-minded" (James 4:8).

Washing this vessel, cleaning out the inside first, He scrubs harder - more water, the smell is gone, the kettle is down to the metal. Now the outside to finally settle, a vessel worthy of being used of Him.

Without God I am:

Getting dirty, but I've grown accustomed to my filth, the smells of anger, feelings of resentment, looks of greed, they all feed an inner need, oh for God to change my lead.

With God I am:

Cleaned up, this vessel stays clean by God's ever-present cup. I drink of His grace and mercy daily to stay in His favor, this vessel to carry blessings to flavor, children of the Savior.

Right Choices:

Ajax won't shine it, Mr. Clean won't clean it, the Tide is in, but I'm still full of sin, it's a twenty mule team pull, and it's going slow. Kind of like a slow cooker, I'm getting tender but full of flavor with the Savior (see 2 Timothy 2:21).

December 17 – God is Near – Firm - Strong

The Bible says, "But because of his great love for us, God, who is rich in mercy, 5made us alive with Christ even when we were dead in transgressions--it is by grace you have been saved" (Ephesians 2:4-5).

Near - firm - strong, He takes my arm, but I feel so alone and afraid of harm, if only I could see His might,
my fright would flee from me, His purpose in-dwelt.

Without God I am:

Alone, to stand the test of time, I've taken this life to be totally mine, yet God has blest and used me, now He calls my life to be used consciously to glorify Him.

With God I am:

Held, in the grip of God's love, mercy, and grace flow to me from above, courage comes from the Son, thank you, Jesus, for what you have done.

Right Choices:

Rich in mercy, when we were dead, saved by grace, it sounds like most would have given up on this soul, being close sometimes is difficult, especially when it is dead. God's not fickle about this; He stands alongside holding us firm, though we are weak (see 2 Chronicles 20:17).

December 18 – God is Broken and Poured Out

The Bible says, "This is my blood of the covenant, which is poured out for many," he said to them. 25"I tell you the truth, I will not drink again of the fruit of the vine until that day when I drink it anew in the kingdom of God" (Mark 14:24-25).

Broken and poured out, His body and blood given for us, that we remember and trust, the purpose for His being, our seeing and believing, called to worship and glorify Him.

Without God I am:

Remembered, for awhile by others, this life I have given to pass, ashes to ashes - dust to dust, my legacy given at last eternally to rust in hell.

With God I am:

Remembering, Christ and what He did for me, His body broken, and His blood poured out, so I could be free from sin's bondage and held captive by Thee.

Right Choices:

Christ's blood poured out, freely to all, in truth, it's all been given, there is no more to drink, the story has been told of Him, what is left is our story, to be shared with Him, may it be, finish well my friend (see 2 Corinthians 8:11).

December 19 – God is Our Inner Peace

The Bible says, "Peace I leave with you; my peace I give you. I do not give to you as the world gives. Do not let your hearts be troubled and do not be afraid" (John 14:27).

My inner peace, when His will becomes my will.

Without God I am:

Stressed, because my will is my will.

With God I am:

At Peace, because my will is His will.

Right Choices:

Don't be troubled or afraid, why? What does Christ give that the world does not? We will not know until we ask Him. His word says, don't let your heart be troubled, easier said than done for sure. The issue here is really who am I going to let deal with this, Him or me? It's an easy answer in my view, but will I do what He is asking me to do? Oh, how he loves you and me (see Isaiah 52:7)!

December 20 – God is Making Us Anew

The Bible says, "and have put on the new self, which is being renewed in knowledge in the image of its Creator" (Colossians 3:10).

Making us anew, like fresh winds blowing through our inner mind, to find the blemish that is mine, desire gone but not for long, Lord - keep me strong.

Without God I am:

Born, into life's struggles that seem not fair, resentment and selfish pride come from where I barely understand. If only I can have the courage for one more day - oh to pray.

With God I am:

Born, into life's struggles that quicken me to call, on a life partner whose mightiness is tall, steadfast, sure, in stealth. He's leading me to wealth in spirit, joy, and health.

Right Choices:

This is a total remake. The problem is it won't happen in just one take. I'm hanging on to the person of old because I feel the most comfortable in this old mold (see Romans 9:20).

December 21 – God is Our Calvary

The Bible says, "Jesus said to her, "I am the resurrection and the life. He who believes in me will live, even though he dies; 26and whoever lives and believes in me will never die. Do you believe this" (John 11:25-26)?

Our Calvary, He gave His life for all, the only payable toll, able in value to reach, an atonement now that is preached. Given freely but not cheap, It will cost us now to bow deep, giving our life's will to Jesus Christ and what happened on Calvary's hill.

Without God I am:

My Calvary, at the end of my day, I'll have to say, I consumed my time well, but - I'm going to hell, if only now I could tell, this Jesus who knows me well, come - forgive me, spare me eternal hell.

With God I am:

His Calvary, He died as though only for me, His precious life given for me, as payment for all my sin has rent, now I relent -spent to be - His glory Divine - fine.

Right Choices:

Calvary, a place and occurrence of an act, few understand and even fewer own, pray about this today (see Romans 1:4).

DECEMBER 22 – GOD IS OUR POINT MAN

The Bible says, "And when the centurion, who stood there in front of Jesus, heard his cry and saw how he died, he said, "Surely this man was the Son of God"" (Mark 15:39)!

Our point man, His presence, plan, and power confront our stubborn wills, taking our difficulties caused by not following His ideal will. He takes our confession in prayer and welds all that is there, into something ultimately good.

Without God I am:

My point man, left alone to contend, Satan was my friend, but now abandoned in my sin. If only I would come to Him, I'm left alone and deceived by all my greed, to deal alone with all my needs - yet Jesus the rock stands at this door and knocks.

With God I am:

His Point man, my only ultimate purpose and goal with this gifted life, to be obedient to His will and glorify Him, my redeemer and friend.

Right Choices:

The lead man, driving through all obstacles, all He asks is that we take His hand (see Deuteronomy 32:4).

DECEMBER 23 – GOD IS ACCEPTING US

The Bible says, "and be found in him, not having a righteousness of my own that comes from the law, but that which is through faith in Christ--the righteousness that comes from God and is by faith" (Philippians 3:9).

Accepting us, where we are, though we have wandered far, His total understanding of me offers hope because He created me. His love is healing us from every scar of mistrust, trusting now in Him, wanting not to sin.

Without God I am:

Accepted, in my own mind for, who I am, sometimes I wonder - who is this man? My actions out of sync with what I think and what I really believe has taken leave in a blink.

With God I am:

Accepted, as a feeble, mistrusted, sinful, selfish, and sorrowful soul. Who has seen the light, and to my delight, this Jesus embraces all that I am, saying - with me you can, be the man in the plan.

Right Choices:

Too often, I feel like He is rejecting me, simply can't measure up, where is this message coming from? Not from Him (see Romans 12:1).

December 24 – God is Zealous

The Bible says, "The LORD said to Moses, 11"Phinehas son of Eleazar, the son of Aaron, the priest, has turned my anger away from the Israelites; for he was as zealous as I am for my honor among them, so that in my zeal I did not put an end to them" (Numbers 25:10-11).

Zealous, passionate with ardent fervor about His love for us, a love unequaled, misunderstood and lacking trust because our sin keeps our heart hidden within.

Without God I am:

Zealous, about me being first, the best and most satisfied of all thirst.

With God I am:

Zealous, when my eyes can see what my heart can feel, and my mind understand, this Jesus so fine - taking my hand, revealing His plan - one day at a time - sublime.

Right Choices:

Zealousness is being driven with a passion for an outcome that is worthy to behold. God knows what is good for me, my problem is I tend to flee from what is really good for me (see Proverbs 23:17).

December 25 – God is Single Hearted

The Bible says, "I will give them singleness of heart and action, so that they will always fear me for their own good and the good of their children after them" (Jeremiah 32:39).

Single hearted, pure in purpose, always the same, unchanging is His name - Savior - Lord - Counselor - Friend - Judge - Warrior - Holy King.

Without God I am:

Dual hearted, heir of a natural nature to sin, serving
needs that come from within, a broken heart from the start,
Jesus came and did His part, to put us back together again.

With God I am:

Dual hearted, my eyes long to see what my heart struggles to feel. This sinful nature inside is meeting a holy God who abides, one thought away from a Heavenly Father, who empowers victory over sin.

Right Choices:

Christmas day, and the subject is being "single-hearted." God gave His only begotten Son, how single-hearted is that (see Hebrews 5:5)?

December 26 – God is Counselor

The Bible says, "For to us a child is born, to us a son is given, and the government will be on his shoulders. And he will be called Wonderful Counselor, Mighty God, Everlasting Father, Prince of Peace" (Isaiah 9:6).

Counselor, when we take the time, stop on a dime, and say, Lord, I can't get there from here, I need you near.

Without God I am:

Counseled, by what seems best, my vision has a crest, not far enough for me to see, the path that will lead me free.

With God I am:

Counseled, by God's saints and His Holy Spirit, I love to read His holy Word and let it seed, sensitive to His call,
each day I pray for where to serve Him with my all.

Right Choices:

Yes, a child is born, Prince of Peace, oh what a feast! Mighty Counselor, what do I need to tell Him, ask Him, pray to Him, care for Him, and a friend? A friend whom I know does not know that I know that he knows nothing about Jesus. Lord, help me to be bold and humble (see Isaiah 5:19).

DECEMBER 27 – GOD IS JEALOUS

The Bible says, "The LORD is a jealous and avenging God; the LORD takes vengeance and is filled with wrath. The LORD takes vengeance on his foes and maintains his wrath against his enemies" (Nahum 1:2).

Jealous, when my love for Him grows dim, and my love for sin grows greater within, this Friend abandoned is hurt, because I've chosen dirt, over His amazing, great worth.

Without God I am:

Jealous, when my eyes see what I cannot hold, yet another has gained what I behold, my greed will lead me to another mistrusted deed.

With God I am:

Jealous, when my feelings about "wants" cause strife and desires get ahead of God's blessings and my "needs".

Right Choices:

It goes to show me how much God really cares, that He would experience feelings of hurt by my actions. How can I do that to Him? I mean, I'm powerless and so insignificant, how can this be? It's easy when I think that He really died for you and me; our names are written on his hand, you see (see 1 Corinthians 10:22).

DECEMBER 28 – GOD IS MIGHTY

The Bible says, "Mightier than the thunder of the great waters, mightier than the breakers of the sea-- the LORD on high is mighty" (Psalm 93:4).

Mighty, such a small word for such a big God, not one thing can thwart Him, be for but never against, this God who is our defense.

Without God I am:

Mighty, like the sandcastle, built too close to the incoming tide. Our choices will decide how mightily we will ride.

With God I am:

Mighty, when I walk in the shadow of the glory and grace of God Almighty - amen!

Right Choices:

We have too small a view of God. We don't give Him enough space. The amazing thing is that for a time He lets us get away with it. A day is coming when, as Jeremiah and the prophets of old have said, the sound of glory will be deafening, the sight of His coming beyond words of reckoning (see Deuteronomy 3:24)!

December 29 – God is An Antidote

The Bible says, "Do not be anxious about anything, but in everything, by prayer and petition, with thanksgiving, present your requests to God. 7And the peace of God, which transcends all understanding, will guard your hearts and your minds in Christ Jesus" (Philippians 4:6-7).

An antidote, the venom of Satan's lies, feeds my eyes while my mind takes time to think "this is fine", my spirit in-dwelt by God puts it all in check, to save this life from an ugly wreck.

Without God I am:

Poisoned, from birth with unholy blood, my unrighteousness feeds choices, and the voices of death call my name.

With God I am:

An antidote, holy blood purified by the cross of Christ, redeems this lost soul, which was once lost - but now found.

Right Choices:

Antidote is a thing that counteracts an evil or bad outcome. All it needs is a willing heart, and realizing that if you don't get it, you will surely die a miserable death, get the antidote (see Hebrews 9:14)!

December 30 – God is Redemption

The Bible says, "I have swept away your offenses like a cloud, your sins like the morning mist. Return to me, for I have redeemed you" (Isaiah 44:22).

Redemption, wiped clean with not a trace of distaste,
for who I am now in the eyes of God, I'm humbled at the price - Jesus sacrificed His all.

Without God I am:

Guilty, with a price to pay that will cost eternity.

With God I am:

Innocent, free and fully pardoned.

Right Choices:

Redemption is the process of becoming one with the Lord in holiness. The process requires a lifetime of submission to the enabling power of our creator. It is a willingness to want more of Him, and less of me and my sin. An intentional effort to put priority on not just living, but being in harmony and at peace with my heavenly Father, who loves and cares for me beyond understanding (see Psalm 130:7).

December 31 – God is God

The Bible says, "Who among the gods is like you, O LORD? Who is like you-- majestic in holiness, awesome in glory, working wonders? 12You stretched out your right hand and the earth swallowed them. 13"In your unfailing love you will lead the people you have redeemed. In your strength you will guide them to your holy dwelling" (Exodus 15:11-13).

God - Amen!

Without God I am:

Lost - Amen!

With God I am:

Saved - Amen!

Right Choices:

God is in monotheistic religions, the creator and ruler of the universe, regarded as eternal, infinite, all-powerful, and all-knowing; supreme being; almighty and everlasting. This is my B-Day! My hope and prayer is that along this journey in this devotional, He has given you a new birth, new hope, and a new day to be all He would have you be...Amen (see Ephesians 1:7)!

PRAYER OF SUBMISSION

Dear Jesus,

Today I confess my sinful nature and ask that you renew my mind and forgive me for my sinfulness. I have rebelled dearly against your desires for my life.

I acknowledge and believe you are my Savior and that your Holy Spirit is here to be my Counselor, indwelling my entire being. Come Lord Jesus and be my Savior, guide and direct my life and help me to confess anew each day my need for forgiveness and desire to serve God.

Help me, Jesus, to be thankful in all my circumstances, knowing now the peace that passes all understanding in Christ Jesus.

Amen

ACKNOWLEDGMENTS:

Pastor Don Brekhus served as a Lutheran pastor for forty three years. He has pastored in four parishes in North Dakota, Oregon, and Washington (two) of which were over 1000 members). He is a true brother in Christ, near and dear. We grew up on farms across the river from each other, and he is a soul mate, a friend for eternity.

An angel brought John Hays into this project at the end to add quality and clarity with edits to the manuscript. I am deeply indebted to this humble man for his service and friendship.

ABOUT THE AUTHOR

Jack A. Madson   www.dailyredemption.com

I grew up on a dairy farm in the Pacific Northwest. It was a small farm community where people helped one another, cared for one another, never locked a door, or took the keys out of the car. Growing up in this rural area in the 50s helped me appreciate family and close friends.

We attended the Lutheran church as a family, confirmation classes, Sunday school, Sunday afternoon with the cousins at Grandpa and Grandma's farm with cookies and Kool-Aid in the afternoon.

My view of God was this far off authority that held reverence and respect. It was not relational. I left the family farm when I was 18 and went to work for another farmer who was stricken with arthritis and needed help. Instant freedom was a fantastic experience as I finished high school and started college. It was innocent, and I maintained my anchor in my faith, in-part through very close friends. Relationships do matter and make a difference in our lives. They encourage, guide, and influence what we think and what we do.

I thank the Lord for my young adult friends and one in particular whom I've asked to write an introduction in this book. Pastor Don Brekhus is not only my longest-oldest friend, but he is also my best friend. We would be riding around with shotguns in his pickup truck, looking for ducks, and he would have these Bible verses pasted on the dashboard. I can remember reading them and thinking, boy, he is going over-board here – what's this all about?

College came and the Peace Corps in the middle, with the experience of a lifetime living in Iran in Baluchistan. Again, my faith was tested as I learned to trust the Lord.

My faith grew through this time, and in the late '60s, as I returned to college in San Luis Obispo, California, life was crazy, especially in California. Nearing the end, I made a trip up to Seattle to see family and met another old friend, the daughter of the farmer I had worked for my last year of high school. Kathy and I connected like a couple of old farm kids.

We've been married now over five decades. We've fought hard for our marriage. We learned how to extend grace to one another, just as the Lord does. The providence of God has stood by us and kept it together. As our family grew up, we kept involved in church activities, building our faith and trust in the Lord Jesus.

Later in my career, my life took a challenging turn. I kept re-inventing my professional identity and lost track of my spiritual identity. I made terrible choices that turned everything upside down.

I put the brakes on life and did not work at any job for a full year. The Lord put me on a "project," to learn about Him through His word and draw deep into his well of grace and restoration. About that time, a good friend of mine, Rae Mackay, was dying of cancer, and as I talked over this project, he helped me form the structure around life "with" and "without" God. The "panels" have been a work-in-progress for the past 18 years, reading, praying over, and claiming back lost ground.

Building a relationship with anyone takes time, and the one with the Lord is extraordinary for each of us. It's to be treasured like gold and sought after as a panhandler on the Klondike. Choices are so important; the Lord gives them to us every day. The best ones get made with Him standing close.

May the Lord be your closest partner in this journey through life as you write your story and build your future eternity with the Lord God Almighty!

Blessings,
Jack A Madson
Poulsbo, Washington
www.dailyredemption.com